"Reading *Hope When It's Hard* was ... Adoption is not for the faint of heart, ... struggles. Jennifer does a beautiful job of capturing the fears, worries, excitement, pain, and hope that come during the adoption process, all the while pointing us directly to Jesus and His glorious Word. Whether you have adopted, know someone who is adopting, plan to adopt, or simply have a heart for adoption, this book will undoubtedly be a blessing to you too!"
    —HEATHER PLATT, wife to Dr. David Platt (author of *Radical*) and mom of four incredible children (including two who joined the family through adoption)

"Jennifer Phillips is one of the most qualified authors to write on the subject of adoption."
    —WALES GOEBEL, founder of Lifeline Children's Service and Sav-A-Life, sex and family education

"The journey of adoption . . . more joy, more fear, more *everything* than you realized you signed on for. You need Jesus, and you need a friend who gets it because she's been there. You have such a friend in Jennifer Phillips. Don't let her winsome manner and sharp wit fool you; she'll draw you in and go straight to the heart of the matter. You'll leave these pages feeling seen, understood, and, most of all, drawn to the Father."
    —JULIE SPARKMAN, executive director of Restore Counseling Ministries

"I've prayed, dreamed, and longed for the book you now hold in your hands. The God who awaits you in these pages answered that prayer through my friend Jennifer Phillips. This is a powerful, honest, and beautiful devotional for families who have adopted, fostered, or contemplated either. In these pages, you will be captivated by a God who pursues you daily, combating your orphan mentality and heart with His work of grace."
    —HERBIE NEWELL, president and executive director of Lifeline Children's Services

"*Hope When It's Hard* is a raw and inspiring look at the journey of adoption. As an adoptive parent, I was encouraged by the sense of community sparked by Jennifer's honest words. *Hope When It's Hard* is an encouragement and a joyful reminder of the gospel."
    —SARA W. BERRY, CEO of Bethel Road Publications and author of *A Broken Mirror*

"It is rare to find a resource for parents that is authentic about the joys and challenges of the adoption journey. Though it is not easy, this devotional reminds each of us that it is worth it to press in and press forward."
    —TERRI COLEY, director of pre- and post-adoption support and founding board member of Show Hope

"Jennifer Phillips's passion for orphans and adoption comes straight from the heart of God. When it's sometimes easier to think only of yourself and your family, her book is a living reminder that God's Word calls us to care for those without a home. God works through adoption, and Jennifer reminds us that we are to be His hands and feet of compassion. It is only by His grace we are able to give those who do not know the love of parents a new life full of family and acceptance."
    —TERRY W. SHARP, state, association, and diaspora network leader of the International Mission Board, SBC

"Jennifer Phillips has written the perfect devotional for couples who are walking through the adoption process or contemplating the adoption journey. With a commitment to honest storytelling and the ability to weave Scripture into her narratives, Phillips brings home the realities of what can happen when you open your heart and home to adoption. She reminds us that adoption itself is a beautiful core truth that every believer has experienced, wrapped around the gospel of Jesus Christ."
—KATHY CHAPMAN SHARP, author of *Life's Too Short to Miss the Big Picture for Women*

"As I read *Hope When It's Hard*, I caught myself being sucked into a more loving understanding of my relationship with my own heavenly Father. Could it be that this devotional is for much more than just adoptive families? I give this question a wholehearted *yes!* And if it could be that rich for someone who hasn't adopted a child, how much richer could it be for those who have the tangible right before them?"
—ANNA NASH, founder and director of Beacon People and author of *pathFinder: A Journey Towards Purpose*

"Adoption is one of the scriptural images used to describe our relationship to God, affirming God's choice of us as His children (Romans 8:15). Jennifer affirms the beauty of the adoptive relationship. Many devotionals are long on inspiration but short on scriptural affirmation. That is not the case with this book. It is a must-read for every adoptive parent and any couple considering adoption."
—KEN HEMPHILL, founding director of North Greenville University's Center for Church Planting and Revitalization

"Jennifer Phillips has identified key biblical truths that speak specifically and personally to adoptive families in a way that, if embraced, will provide instruction and inspiration to guide their steps through the entire adoption process."
—CHARLES A. FOWLER, senior pastor of Germantown Baptist Church, Germantown, TN

"Adopting a child internationally can often be a challenging experience. While the end result is a precious child, the road often feels long and lonely. Jennifer Phillips walked this path with grace and hope. She now sets out to encourage those coming behind her on this amazing journey with this incredible devotional."
—KARLA THRASHER, China program director for Lifeline Children's Services

"This devotional is so very needed in the adoption community. This process can be so tiring, joyful, exhausting, and even lonely at times. Families for sure go through a stretching of faith when they go through this journey. Jennifer lays out just the right encouragement and spiritual hope we all need in this journey we call adoption."
—KELLEY CLAYTON BERRY, founder of Touch the Sky and mom of five (including three who joined the family through adoption)

HOPE WHEN IT'S HARD

30 DAYS OF HOPE
FOR ADOPTIVE PARENTS

JENNIFER PHILLIPS

NEW HOPE®
PUBLISHERS
Gospel-Centered. Missions-Driven.

BIRMINGHAM, ALABAMA

New Hope® Publishers
100 Missionary Ridge
Birmingham, AL 35242
NewHopePublishers.com
An imprint of Iron Stream Media
IronStreamMedia.com

Iron Stream Media serves its authors as they express their views, which may not express the views of the publisher.

A previous edition of Hope When It's Hard was filed as
Library of Congress Cataloging-in-Publication Data
Names: Phillips, Jennifer, 1977- author.
Title: 30 days of hope for adoptive parents / by Jennifer Phillips.
Other titles: Thirty days of hope for adoptive parents
Description: First Edition. | Birmingham, Alabama : New Hope Publishers, 2016.
Identifiers: LCCN 2016039467 (print) | LCCN 2016041024 (ebook) | ISBN
    9781625915153 (permabound) | ISBN 9781596699687 (Ebook)
Subjects: LCSH: Adoptive parents--Religious life. | Adoptive parents--Prayers
    and devotions. | Adoption--Religious aspects--Christianity. |
    Hope--Religious aspects--Christianity.
Classification: LCC BV4529.15 .P45 2016 (print) | LCC BV4529.15 (ebook) | DDC
248.8/45--dc23
LC record available at https://lccn.loc.gov/2016039467

ISBN-13: 978-1-56309-420-0
Ebook ISBN: 978-1-56309-421-7

1 2 3 4 5—24 23 22 21 20

For Mom, the most selfless person I know.

Contents

Acknowledgments

I like to joke that I'm an "accidental author." Although writing has long been a passion of mine, I always thought of book writing as a far-off dream, as in, "In another life, I'd like to be an author." But God had other plans, and He used a lot of good people along the way to get me to this place of being a published writer.

Thank you, Mrs. Rouse, my 12th grade AP English teacher, for drilling those five-paragraph essays like it was your job (wait—it was your job!), and encouraging my willingness to think deeply about rich literature.

Thank you, Dad, for seeing something special in my writing from an early age, and paying ridiculous amounts in international postage to send me really heavy writing books because you wanted to push me to pursue my dreams. Thank you for editing and praising my work, while also being willing to say, "This isn't quite right; you can do better." Thank you, Mom, for supporting me like only a mama can.

Thank you, Faithful Fifty, who were the selected readers of my first blog—a blog I kept "invitation only" because I was too scared to let too many people see my heart. Thank you for reading when I really didn't know what I was doing. Thanks for telling me that my words impacted your life.

Thank you, readers of my *Bringing Lucy Home* blog, now jenniferphillipsblog.com. Thank you for hanging on my every word during our adoption immigration crisis and for asking me to keep writing, long after the drama had passed.

Thank you to all who have read and championed my book, *Bringing Lucy Home.* Your kind, generous words and five-star reviews helped me to realize, "Wait a minute. I think writing is actually what I was made to do. *This brings me so much life.*"

Thank you, New Hope Publishers, for reaching out to me and giving me such an incredible opportunity to do, on a large scale, something that I love to do in day-to-day life: encourage adoptive families with truth from God's Word. This book has been an honor to write, and you have taken such good care of me in the process.

Thank you, Lifeline Children's Services, for not only walking with us in our journey to Lucy, but for advocating for orphans worldwide and uniting so many with forever families.

Thank you, Brian, for being incredibly patient as I spent all my nights and all of Lucy's naptimes writing, writing, writing. It means so much that you value my gifts and passions, even if they cause me to drop a lot of other balls. Thank you Joshua, Andrew, Sarah Kate, and Lucy, for being the best kids ever. I love our messy, imperfect life, and I love that we all know that it's OK to be messy and imperfect. I could not be more proud of each of you.

Thank you, Jesus, for the hope of the gospel, without which I would be utterly lost. I pray that my words bring You much honor and glory.

Introduction

My heart beat out of my chest as the Chinese nanny rounded the corner, cradling an infant in layers upon layers of clothing. "Lian Yonghui!" a voice announced. This name—her orphanage name but no longer her name—danced in my ears, declaring that the moment had finally arrived. There she was—our Lucy Mei, our "beautiful light."

You could say this is where our story began, this day we became a family of six instead of five and jumped headfirst into a deep well of endless joy and challenges we could never have anticipated. Yet, this life-changing event was more like a climactic chapter in an even greater story. The narrative truly began months, even years, before when God began orchestrating events and desires that eventually led us to a chilly day in a government office in southern China when time stood still. When hope became reality.

But the account didn't end there. Many chapters ensued, documenting rejection, grief, and loss, baby steps, hints of trust, affection denied, and affection received. We celebrated attachment as our hearts sang, "I would lay my life down for you!" We felt despair as we had to admit, "This is harder than I ever imagined." Our adoption story details siblings cheering their sister on as she learned to eat, stand, walk, and speak. It shares how those same brothers and sister sometimes struggle with sharing their space, hearts, and parents.

And the story continues. Countless chapters have yet to be written.

You could say the adoption journey is a long, winding road. Sometimes the scenery is breathtaking and you think, "There is no place I would rather be." You take off your shoes and worship because the transformations that take place within your heart, your child, and your home are simply miraculous. Yet, as is the case with most long trips, the view might sometimes be dull and monotonous, clouded with paperwork and waiting and milestones that refuse to be crossed.

The terrain can also be unchartered, treacherous, and terrifying. You may not see another soul for miles and you wonder, "Am I the only one who feels this way?" And then the fog clears, colors splash across the sky as hope and progress emerge, and you find yourself in awe once again of the enormous privilege this pilgrimage actually is.

I don't know where you are in your adoption journey. Maybe you've just started filling out the paperwork. Maybe your children are now in their teens. Perhaps you are battered and bruised, cautiously pursuing adoption on the heels of a lengthy battle with infertility, and you are afraid to hope. Maybe you have a houseful of kids but feel called to make room in your home for one more. Or two. Maybe others think you're crazy for doing so. Maybe you're adopting domestically, or perhaps from a faraway land.

Although each circumstance would warrant its own book, adoption in general creates a unique pattern of victories and struggles that most families experience. One universal truth is this: no matter what chapter your story is on, no matter the particular bend in the road, my guess is that each one of you could use some hope . . . which is why you and I are meeting today. It's why, hopefully, we'll be spending the next thirty days together.

My prayer for this devotional is for you to *be seen* and to *see*. As we go to Scripture each day to tackle the issues involved in pursuing and parenting these treasures of ours, I desire for you to know you are seen—and therefore loved and understood—by our perfect adoptive Father who numbers every hair on our heads and understands even the most secret burdens in our hearts.

And I want you to *see*. I want you to see our God who, in His sovereignty, holds all things together so we don't have to. I want you to see that you, your child, and your whole family are so incredibly cherished and provided for. I want you to see that we have a King who cheers us on and delights in our children. I want you to see that He owns all the resources we'll ever need, thank goodness.

Let's spend thirty gospel-rich days together, shall we? I am in the trenches with you. I understand you. I hurt with you. I am so proud of you. Let's run to Jesus together and drink deeply from the abundant life He promises to give us as we live out this honored calling.

Day 1

OUR STORY
OF ADOPTION

*See what great love the Father has lavished on
us, that we should be called children of God!
And that is what we are!*

—1 John 3:1

*H*ave you ever wondered why God is so passionate about orphans? It's obvious that He is. Scripture overwhelms us with references to His compassion for them and His call to care for them. He "defends the cause of the fatherless" (Deuteronomy 10:18). He commands the Israelites to always leave portions of the harvest for the orphans to gather and promises retribution for those who withhold justice from these little ones (Deuteronomy 24–27). He is intentionally named as a "father to the fatherless" (Psalm 68:5). Scripture even names orphan care as "pure and faultless" religion (James 1:27). Wow—that's strong language!

Why is this? Why is God so head-over-heels crazy about orphans, and why does He defend them so intensely? Why is He specifically concerned about their provision?

Because that's what His people once were.

If you are a follower of Jesus, your relationship with Him had a beginning. It has not always been. Even if you think, "I can't remember a time when I didn't trust Jesus," there was such a time. So how did that relationship begin?

Pursuit. God's beautiful, unrelenting, at-all-costs pursuit of your heart.

God said, "I will say to those called 'Not my people,' 'You are my people'; and they will say, 'You are my God'" (Hosea 2:23). Because He made you and adores you, when you were far off and did not know or care who He was, He came for you. He knew you didn't have much to offer—even the good things you presented were but rags before Him (Isaiah 64:6). But it didn't matter, because He's the King. All the resources of the universe belong to Him. There was no need to impress Him with your performance or pedigree or credentials—He simply wanted you for you, not because of what you could give Him.

So He paid a cost. A great, heavy cost that would have been impossible for you to pay on your own. It was brutal and ugly, but He walked into that suffering with eyes wide open and focused on the prize—you. He knew what was on the other side of that cost: your redemption, complete with a new name and a new home. A secure future. A father—and not just any father, but the only perfect Father there ever will be.

Yes, God adores orphans.

Doesn't that just leave you awestruck? You have a Father who not only loves you but came for you, wooed you, moved heaven and earth—literally—to make you His own. He made a sacrifice beyond comprehension to bring you into His family for good.

Do you know what that kind of radical love gives us? Security. What security we can have when we're tempted to forget our new name! With confidence, we can tell the enemy, "I have a name, and it is not *Forgotten*. It is not *Alone*. It is not *Shame*. My identity lies in the One who came for me, who died for me, who promised never to leave me. You cannot change my name, no matter how hard you try, because it is etched into my Father's hands. I have a forever name spoken by my forever Father from my forever home."

We are orphans no more, and there's not a thing that will ever change that, praise God.

Is earthly adoption a perfect picture of spiritual adoption? No, it can't be. We are not perfect parents, and we cannot change our children's hearts, let alone secure their eternity. But we love without the promise of love in return. We pursue our children before they even know we exist. By God's grace, we have the privilege of gifting, maybe not a new heart but a new name, a new family, and a new home. A new life. While not a perfect analogy, adoption still miraculously pulls back the veil and gives us special insight into the adopting heart of our Father as our love for these treasured ones beats in time with His. The mystery of His great, consuming love for us is revealed just a little bit more as we realize, "The way I love this child—this is a taste of how He loves me! My desire to give even when I get nothing in return—this is how He pursued me! I want to give life to these dull eyes staring at me from the referral picture on my screen—because He gave life to me! This child was not mine, but now he is, just as I am now and forever a child of the King. I can barely comprehend it."

Our only possible response? Worship.

> Father,
> What a privilege it is to call You by that name! I am so overwhelmed that You would love me when I did not love You, when I didn't even know who You were. Thank You for giving me a new heart, a new name, and a new inheritance. When I'm tempted by things in this world, will You remind me of my name? When I start to question where my provision will come from, when I am hesitant to trust, when I am tricked into believing that I am still an orphan left alone in this world, will You whisper truths of identity, safety, and love? Thank You for patiently embracing me as Your own. There is no better Father, no greater protector, no closer friend than You.

Day 2

ADOPTION— A CALLING?

Trust in the LORD with all your heart
and lean not on your own understanding;
in all your ways submit to him,
and he will make your paths straight.

—Proverbs 3:5–6

*W*hen I was a kid I played church league basketball. Before you make any assumptions about my skill level, you need to know that my eight-year-long career high was five points in one game. No, that is not a typo: five.

I did practice, though, bless my heart. Many Friday afternoons before the weekend game, I would shoot hoops in the backyard. Every now and then, I would stop and pray, "OK, God, if You're going to help me to do really well in the game tomorrow, then let me make this next shot." Sometimes I made it; more often than not, I didn't. I never did extremely well in a game.

What was I looking for in those moments? A sign.

We all do it, don't we? Maybe not with basketball, but like Gideon in Judges 6, we set out woolen fleeces, begging God to give us insight into what He's going to do or what He wants us to do. We desperately want to know this mysterious will of His, and we exhaust all human resources to find it. We're afraid that we'll hear or interpret Him incorrectly, and either way our lives will be utterly ruined. My dad calls this the "paralysis of analysis," a diagnosis he gave me when I was trying to choose a course of study in college. I was so terrified of making the wrong decision—of missing God's will for my life—that I just couldn't make any decision at all.

Adoption is a huge decision, one of the biggest decisions you could possibly make. No one can or should make this life-altering choice lightly. Yes, adoption is amazing and God-honoring, but not everyone is called to it. So how do you know you are?

Everyone's story looks different. Some people have always been passionate about orphan care, so it is a natural next step. For others, the desire comes out of the blue. For others still, God uses incredible circumstances to make the adoption path crystal clear, and they respond in obedience, even though they are terrified.

For my husband and me, our decision was made on a park bench after reading through a list of pros and cons. There was no fanfare; lightning did not fall from the sky. Over the previous months and years, as our burden for orphan care increased, we examined means of grace such as God's Word and the body of Christ. We also considered our own passions and gifting, as well as our circumstances. We knew from Scripture that God champions adoption, the body affirmed our desire to adopt as a good thing, and God opened a door for us to adopt as Americans living in Australia, something we did not think was possible.

Even though all the evidence seemed to flash *go*, we still weren't 100 percent sure. What if we got it wrong? How could we know for sure that this was what we were supposed to do? We were talking about a human being's life, for goodness' sake, not to mention the potential to rock the stability of what was then our family.

In the end, all we could pray was, "God, we think this is what You're calling us to do. We think this is where You're leading us. So, we're going to take the next step. If we're wrong, please stand in the way. We're stepping out in faith here, so we're trusting that You'll honor our desire to obey, no matter which way You lead us."

And with that prayer, on a park bench in a quiet suburban neighborhood, we said yes.

How often do we miss out on incredible opportunities because we don't want to act until we're 100 percent sure? God's will—His power and rule over our lives—is so much bigger and wider than the tightrope walk we like to think it is. We wobble fearfully, knees knocking, terrified to take a step lest we fall off the rope entirely and wreck God's entire cosmic scheme—*as if we could do that*—and we miss out on so much. The paralysis of "What if I get it wrong?" leaves us stagnant, with dormant dreams as discolored and irrelevant as a yellowed keepsake in a cedar chest.

"Trust Me," He says. *"Trust Me."* If the desire of our hearts is to know and follow Him, we just can't get it wrong. Trust Him to open doors. Trust Him to stand in your way. You may not be completely sure that you're called to adopt, but start walking—listening the whole time, asking for guidance, asking for assurance, and trusting, trusting, trusting. Rarely do we have all the answers, rarely do we have the privilege of seeing the whole picture before-hand, so don't waste time waiting until you do.

If you think God is calling you to adopt, but you're not quite sure, here's what you do: First, immerse yourself daily in His Word. Romans 12:2 says that if we want to know God's will, our minds need to be renewed. God's Word renews our minds. And then? Do the next thing. Take the next step. Trust that God will always bless a heart that wants to obey and that He will direct your steps, either way.

> ## Father,
> My heart's desire is to obey You. I know that there is no better or safer place to be than the center of Your will, but sometimes it's hard to know exactly where that is. Help me to faith-fully saturate my life with Your Word so that my mind can be sharp to discern Your "good, pleasing and perfect will" (Romans 12:2). Help me to listen to You; help me to surrender to Your dreams for me. Give me courage to take the next step even when I'm not completely sure of what You want me to do. It's so com-forting to know that You are bigger than my human understanding and misinterpretations. Thank You for always honoring a heart that desires to know and walk with You.

Day 3

HIS PLAN,
HIS PROVISION

*And my God will meet all your needs
according to the riches of his glory in Christ Jesus.*

—Philippians 4:19

God recognized my propensity toward "faith amnesia." He knew, in advance, about my habit of gazing a little too long at challenging circumstances and forgetting His past provision. Maybe that's why He's given me such incredible examples of His faithfulness. He knew that I would need help remembering who I am—a well-provided-for child of the King.

It began with a trip to China during college, a monthlong adventure that involved introducing students to English, basketball, and the Father. My parents gave me permission to go, as long as God provided the money. "If the money comes in, then you'll know that this is what God wants you to do," my dad said.

Week after week, I watched my team members report the progress of their fundraising, as my record sheet remained blank. I continued to attend those training sessions in faith, all the while wondering if I was foolish to hold on to hope. Then the checks began pouring in, one after the other, from known and unknown sources. Before I knew it, I had $1,000 more than I needed. In the end, the girl with the empty record sheet was actually able to support other members of her team because God provided in excess.

If that story wasn't enough, God continues to provide as my husband and I serve in a college ministry with an organization that is 100 percent support based. Sixteen years in, He has never let us down—and yet I still nervously watch those income numbers every December.

God provides for us big time, and yet I still worried about taking on a $30,000 adoption bill. How could we say yes when we had no idea where that money would come from? We certainly didn't have thousands of dollars lying around. Would it be irresponsible to commit to pursuing a child without being sure that we could pay the fees involved?

In this season of faith amnesia, God reminded me that rarely does He tell us every detail of a plan before He calls us to commit to it. He repeated the exhortation He's challenged me with throughout my life: "Jennifer, I own the cattle on a thousand hills. Is $30,000 too much for me? Step out in faith, and watch what I do."

So I did. He answered by providing what we needed and then some. We traveled to China with our adoption paid in full and not a penny in debt. God did that.

God loves to show off in the area of provision! Adoptive families in particular often get the special privilege of having their faith and finances stretched to the max and then seeing their King meet their needs right on time. Here's Kelley's story:

....

After adopting two from China in less than 11 months, we were a bit financially drained and figured we were done. God showed me a little boy who I knew in my heart was supposed to join our family. The only issue was the "how." We had not one penny to start another adoption. Within days of saying yes, friends provided enough to start our home study. We knew right then this process would be a walk of faith like we had never experienced before. Each time we needed to pay a fee, the Lord provided through a fund-raiser we held or a grant we applied for. I believe the Lord had us start the process with no funds whatsoever so that we would totally rely on Him, watch Him provide, and give Him the glory when He came through. The journey taught us so much about His love for us, His love for these children, and the ways He can write a story of provision into our lives that can be shared for a lifetime. God's heart is for these children! All we have to do is take that step of faith and say yes.

....

A story of provision that can be shared for a lifetime. What a gift these stories are! Just like God told the Israelites to create altars of remembrance when He rescued them in battle or provided for them in special ways, God's provision in adoption—whether financially, emotionally, or physically—gives us reasons to set up our own altars and worship.

(See Genesis 28:18–19; 33:20; 35:1–3; Exodus 17:8–16; 24:4; and Joshua 4:1–9 for the Altars of Remembrance passages.)

Are you in a season of faith amnesia? Is God calling you to step into the great unknown, and you just can't see how He'll provide? Look back at what He's done—go back to those altars and *remember*. Then ask Him for what you need because He's a good Father who loves to give good gifts to His children. Have you recently seen God's faithfulness in huge, tangible ways? Set up an altar and *worship*. You'll need that story of provision to strengthen your faith on weaker days.

Tim Keller once tweeted, "The only person who dares wake up a king at 3:00 a.m. for a glass of water is a child. We have that kind of access." Do you have a need? Does it seem like a huge, there's-no-way-this-is-possible kind of a need? Ask Him. Ask Him! Then sit back and watch what the King—your Father, the King— does. The seemingly insurmountable is actually an opportunity for God's awesome provision to take center stage.

Father,
Your resources have no end. Forgive my anxiety. Forgive my tendency to try to meet needs with my own resources—resources that are limited and quickly run out. Thank You for the ways You have faithfully provided for me. They are too many to number. Help me to look back and remember Your faithfulness on the days when my faith is small. And when You provide in miraculous ways, when Your glory is on full display, remind me to set up altars and worship so that I can return to those places when I forget that You really are for me, that You never call me to something for which You do not equip and provide. Thank You for giving me everything I need and more.

Day 4

THE WAITING GAME

Hope deferred makes the heart sick.

—Proverbs 13:12

*I*t's been said that God answers prayers in three different ways: yes, no, and wait. "No" may appear to be the hardest answer to receive, but I personally think "not yet" feels even worse. As my little Lucy likes to say, "It's just so hard to wait, Mama."

"Yes, sweetheart, it is."

Adoptive parents know a thing or two about waiting, don't we? We're always waiting for the next email or phone call from the social worker with news that another step has been accomplished. We wait for a referral, wait to be chosen, wait for this approval and that approval, wait to travel. We wait to hear our child's name called out in a crowded government building. We wait to get to the next step of waiting.

Social media makes the waiting even harder because we can easily compare others' progress with our own:

> *"Her letter of approval came in two weeks—*
> *why have I already waited five?"*

> *"That family was matched almost instantly*
> *and we've waited for years. What's wrong with us?"*

> *"We started this process the same time they did—*
> *how are we so far behind?"*

Oh, it's hard to wait, especially after you see that face for the first time and the hypothetical becomes a living, breathing reality. When you've prepared a beautiful room bursting with comfort and life, it's hard to wait, knowing your little one still sleeps on wooden slats. It's not easy to imagine your sweet one going to bed at night with an empty, aching belly, waiting on paperwork to be approved, when your own pantry is overflowing with nourishing food. Waiting is excruciating when your arms are outstretched, ready to embrace one for whom affection is a foreign concept. Waiting feels cruel when all you've ever wanted to be is a mama and unexpected obstacles stand in the way.

Waiting is never what we would choose, especially when each day's delay means one less day that your chosen one will experience the healing power of love.

But God is in the waiting, isn't He? Yes, even in the waiting—especially in the waiting—He is for our children, and He is for us.

Our friends the Israelites persevered for hundreds of years as slaves in Egypt, and when they were finally granted freedom, God threw open the gates to the Promised Land and told them to run straight in and claim their inheritance. Right? Well, not exactly.

The Israelites were forced to wander. And wait. And wander some more. Forty years to be exact—forty years in the scorching desert, with nothing but mysterious food to eat and no clear destination or ETA. This four-decade-long meandering probably felt like a pointless exercise, especially since God had just enacted the most elaborate rescue plan to date. He literally constructed two gigantic walls of water with a spoken word, ushered His people across the dry sea floor, and drowned the Egyptian army to extract His beloved from bondage. Sure, the Israelites struggled with grumbling and disobedience, but wouldn't God just want them to take a victory lap and enter the winner's circle as quickly as possible?

Yet there was purpose in the waiting:

Remember how the Lord your God led you all the way in the wilderness those forty years, to humble and test you in order to know what was in your heart, whether or not you would keep His commands. He humbled you, causing you to hunger and then feeding you with manna, which neither you nor your ancestors had known, to teach you that man does not live on bread alone, but on every word that comes from the mouth of the Lord.
—Deuteronomy 8:2–3

In the desert, waiting and wandering, God's people had nothing to depend on except Him. All comforts were stripped away, and anything they could possibly cling to, put their hope in, or take credit for didn't exist anymore. Their hearts were exposed.

I wonder: when all you know is stripped away, when circumstances are out of your control, what bubbles out of your heart? I can tell you what my heart reveals: Panic. Anxiety. Distrust. Jealousy for the driver's seat. Despair.

Sometimes the only way for us to recognize how little we trust is for our neat and tidy plans to be pulled out from beneath us.

What did the Israelites learn after humility forced their hearts on display? They learned that they didn't need fancy food to live; they needed His Word. They realized that they didn't need control; they needed Him. And He kept His promise—He led them and provided for them. He did not leave them alone.

> *Your clothes did not wear out and your feet did not*
> *swell during these forty years. Know then in your*
> *heart that as a man disciplines his son, so the LORD*
> *your God disciplines you.*
> *—Deuteronomy 8:4–5*

The Israelites' waiting was not in vain, and neither is ours. The wandering days, months, and years that seem so pointless are actually vital to our spiritual growth. In his book *New Morning Mercies*, Paul David Tripp says, "Be careful how you make sense of your life. What looks like a disaster may in fact be grace." Seeds of desperation yield fruits of humility and deeper dependence on the Provider. Approved paperwork is not the answer; He is. A fast-tracked process does not satisfy; His Word does.

Be careful not to wish away the waiting. Our human understanding may scream, "We're losing precious time!" but God knows that delays are His gifts of sweet mercy—unexpected opportunities to lean in, learn, and be fed with what we actually need: Him.

Father,

Your ways are not my ways, and Your timetable is not my timetable. Forgive me for wishing away the wandering days, the waiting phase. Forgive me for refusing to submit to the fact that even delays are a part of Your good plan for me. Help me to trust You as the Author of my days. Help me to be a willing student of "the wait," anxious to learn all that You want to teach me in these foggy times. Thank You for patiently loving me back to surrender when I try to force Your hand with my own plans and dreams. You are sovereign, and You are good.

Day 5

WHAT ABOUT DOUBTS?

*Whoever wants to be my disciple
must deny themselves and take up their cross
daily and follow me.*

—Luke 9:23

*W*hen our family was preparing to move to Australia to do college ministry, some wise friends who had gone before us shared an insightful analogy they heard from Missions Training International. They said that moving overseas is like walking across a swinging bridge: You leave what's safe and secure and step out onto a wobbly, seemingly dangerous surface. When the wind starts to blow and the bridge begins to shake, you want to run back to solid ground. To normal. To what you know. If you'll just keep walking, you will eventually reach solid ground on the other side. But you have to keep walking.

Truer words have never been spoken. I can't count the number of times before we moved, and even afterwards, that I just wanted to run back to what I knew. I craved solid ground, and nothing about transitioning to the other side of the world felt secure.

The adoption journey is also a shaky, shaky bridge, is it not?

It goes something like this: Life feels stable, safe, and secure—the Triple S's that the world says we should strive for—and then our hearts are stirred. We say yes to pursuing a child who is not our own. We take a step off the platform. Despite the hope of eventual stability, of a new normal, winds of doubt begin to blow and the bridge starts to sway. The new normal seems so far away, and what if we never get there anyway? We look back. The platform is inviting; safety beckons. Maybe we should turn around and go back to what we know. After all, if we were definitely doing the right thing by pursuing adoption, wouldn't we feel more certain?

My husband and I wondered this very thing.

The day we received Lucy's file—the day our future daughter's identity was revealed—was supposed to be one of the happiest days of my life. I had envisioned how it would all go down: The phone would ring. Our social worker would share the happy news. I would scream with excitement and then sob tears of joy when we saw her face on the computer screen for the first time.

My reaction was exactly what I had dreamed it would be—except it was the opposite. Instead of elation I felt grief; joy was nowhere to be found because fear had pushed it out of the scene. I felt heavy, burdened, and so incredibly afraid. We were ruining our family! Our children would resent us! Our motives for adopting were somehow impure, and we hadn't heard from the Lord at all!

Surely this doubt, this heaviness meant we had gotten it wrong. If this child was God's good and perfect plan for our family, there's no way I would feel as if a sack of bricks had suddenly been heaped on my shoulders. Right?

But sometimes God's will is a heavy load. In fact, Jesus said if we're going to follow Him, we have to not only lift, but also carry our cross as we walk. Every single day.

I wonder . . . why didn't Jesus say we only have to take up our cross at salvation? That would make so much more sense to me! That way, when we submit to Jesus, we could lay down our old selves and pick up His Cross, identify with His suffering, and then we could be released to lay it down again and walk pain free.

But Jesus knew that life is hard and our flesh is weak. He knew that we would need constant encouragement to do hard things—things that feel heavy and insurmountable, but reap eternal rewards. He knew that we would need weight on our shoulders to remind us of the cost, to know that the cost is worth it.

Should we dismiss all doubts as invalid? No. Sometimes God creates uneasiness. Sometimes we have gotten it wrong and we need to back up. But more often than not, doubts are just gentle reminders that we must count the cost one more time. God allows us to feel the weight of the Cross—the heaviness of our death to self, of His sacrifice—so that we can surrender anew, desperate for Him to walk the hard road with us. And then we can keep on walking, knowing that joy lies before us in this life and the next.

The joy did come. As we felt the heaviness of our decision, bore the weight of unknown risks and potential heartache, we surrendered anew to this sweet calling. We put one foot in front of the other and gladly said, "Yes. *A thousand times yes.* We choose this little one today and every day after that. She is beautiful and she is ours." Doubts still danced across my mind from time to time, but instead of invoking fear, they pushed me to trust more fully and worship more intensely as I died a little more to self and welcomed into my heart a little more of the unconditional, sacrificial love of Jesus.

Are you in a season of doubt, friend? Talk to your Father about it. He wants to hear you. Maybe He's cautioning you, so lean in and listen close. But maybe, just maybe, He wants you to feel the cost and choose to keep on walking with a heart newly committed to knowing Him in His life and in His death.

> Father,
> The road I'm walking is scary and unknown. I'm afraid; I'm unsettled and unsure. Thank You that my doubts are safe with You and that You are big enough to handle my fears and my temptations to run back to what's familiar. If You are cautioning me, please make that clear. I trust You to do so. But if not, please help me to count the cost and keep walking even when the ground gets shaky. Thank You that even when my circumstances are uncertain, Your promise to remain with me is secure.

Day 6

WHEN OTHERS AREN'T ON BOARD

Bear with each other and forgive one another
if any of you has a grievance against someone.
Forgive as the Lord forgave you.
And over all these virtues put on love,
which binds them all together in perfect unity.

—Colossians 3:13–14

I'll never forget the first time we told a group of people that we were adopting. These were friends who had known us for a while and were special to our family. We waited until the very end of our time together. My husband Brian and I exchanged excited, knowing glances before he let the cat out of the bag:

"Well, we would love your prayers over the next several months because . . . we're adopting!"

The room erupted into whoops, hollers, cheers, tears, and high fives. Friends yelled, "Congratulations!" and wanted to know all the details.

Actually, that's what I thought would happen. How did it go in reality?

Crickets. Absolute silence. I think I heard an eyelash fall onto my cheek. Our elation was met with skepticism, confusion, and caution. *What in the world? Why couldn't they just be happy for us?*

From loved ones to acquaintances, it is inevitable that some people in your life will not fully embrace your decision to adopt. Although you may feel absolutely called to the adoption journey, others may not feel quite so sure for you. They may even be philosophically opposed to adoption. What do you do with what feels like rejection, especially when you are so needy for their support and guidance?

You look to Jesus' example.

If anyone knows what it feels like to be rejected, it's Jesus. His parents were surprised that He would want to preach when He was only a boy (Luke 2:41–50). His brothers didn't believe He was the Messiah until after the Resurrection (John 7:5). He was rejected in His hometown, a wanderer without a pillow to lay His head on (Luke 4:24–30; 9:58). His disciples misinterpreted His parables all the time and refused to accept what He had come to do, even though He implicitly told them He had come to die (Mark 8:27–33). Many of the masses that claimed to support Him only did so because they thought He would free them from Roman rule. Jesus asked His very best friends to remain with Him in His neediest hour and they fell asleep, for crying out loud (Mark 14:37)!

What was Jesus' response to being rejected at the hand of those who were supposed to love Him the most?

Love. Patience. Grace. Forgiveness. Jesus continued to serve those who didn't get Him, patiently displaying His love time and time again, all while continuing to live out His Father's will. He continued to invite them to the table, to invest in their lives and pursue their souls.

What should you do when others don't embrace your decision to adopt? Walk by faith anyway. Respond with grace. Some responses are motivated by love and concern for you, so choose to believe the best about their motivations; you would want someone to give you the same benefit of the doubt. Some people's negative comments are birthed out of misinformation or ignorance. Use their questioning as a platform to rewrite the script in their heads concerning what adoption is and what it is not.

And you know what? Some responses are tied to fears—the same fears you are battling. Your loved ones may question, "How will you cope? How will you pay the adoption fees? What if the process is rocky? What if the child is deeply traumatized? What if there are unknown medical concerns? What if the child rejects you? Have you really thought this through?"

Be gentle in your replies. You have wrestled through these same questions, and if you're honest, you still wrestle with them from time to time. Just as God has stripped you of idols throughout the adoption process, He may very well use your story as a tool of sanctification in others' lives as they are confronted with their own idols of comfort and ease. Humble yourself, admit your own doubts and fears, and testify to the freedom that comes when we lay down the things we thought were dear in exchange for lasting, eternal treasures. Then confess your utter dependence on a God who never calls without equipping, a Father who has promised to make streams in the desert and to never leave you alone (Isaiah 43:19).

Hopefully, your loved ones will eventually jump on board. Or maybe they never will. Regardless, run to the One who understands what it's like to be opposed by those who should love you the most. Lay your heart before Him. He is safe, and He says, "Well done."

Father,

You know what it's like to be rejected. Your followers were fickle and never quite understood what You were up to until You were gone. Yet You loved them anyway. Instead of taking offense and pulling away, You drew them closer. You let not only Your words but every aspect of Your life enforce Your calling. Because of Your secure identity as Your Father's Son, You felt no need to defend Yourself or Your agenda. You simply loved. God, give me the same eyes of love, the same secure identity, the same self-control. Thank You that no matter how others perceive me, I can always find refuge in Your encouragement and love. Help me to be gracious and kind, content in the fact that I am fully known and accepted by You.

Day 7

WRECKED IN THE VERY BEST WAY

I urge you to live a life worthy of the calling you have received.

—Ephesians 4:1

*W*hat dreams do you have for yourself? For your family? I had the greatest group of friends in high school, people I still love and either talk to regularly or connect with via social media. I think of these friends often. I can remember so many late-night, lazy conversations where we tried to imagine our future selves—what we would do, whom we would love. We were Jesus followers and wanted to honor Him, but we also kind of wanted normal lives too—the great marriage, the fulfilling job, the 2.5 kids, the nice house.

Some would say God wrecked those dreams.

My friend Jen is a pastor's wife and a mom of four who has dug the trenches of a church plant, a task that is not for the faint of heart.

Scott and his wife, very settled with two older biological kids, jumped on a plane to China and adopted a three-year-old beauty with special needs.

Dianna got stuck in Uganda for seven weeks as she pleaded daily with the local authorities to let her leave the country with her new son, Job. Inspired by God's battle plan for Joshua at Jericho, she literally walked around the compound where she was staying seven times daily, begging God to tear down the walls of governmental red tape.

And then there's me, their crazy friend who moved her family of five to Australia and then adopted a Chinese baby girl, a process that was anything but smooth.

This is not an exhaustive list.

None of us is exactly living the American dream. Some would say we've exchanged calm, predictable lives for the unpredictable—that we've abandoned security unnecessarily.

But is security really the goal? Should it be the goal?

"Live worthy to the calling you have received," Paul instructed in Ephesians 4:1. What calling have we received in Christ? Jesus had a lot to say about this. Here are just a few of His exhortations:

> *You are the light of the world. A town built on a*
> *hill cannot be hidden. Neither do people light a*

lamp and put it under a bowl. Instead they put it on its stand, and it gives light to everyone in the house. In the same way, let your light shine before others, that they may see your good deeds and glorify your Father in heaven. —Matthew 5:14–16

Do not store up for yourselves treasures on earth, where moths and vermin destroy, and where thieves break in and steal. But store up for yourselves treasures in heaven, where moths and vermin do not destroy, and where thieves do not break in and steal. For where your treasure is, there your heart will be also. —Matthew 6:19–21

Greater love has no one than this: to lay down one's life for one's friends. —John 15:13

God's calling? Opposite of the American dream, but surpassingly greater, don't you think?

Without exception, adoption is guaranteed to rock your seemingly ordered world. You might crave routine and predictability, but the adoption process, and then parenting an adopted child, is the opposite of predictable order. You may feel like you run the risk of shaking up your already established family. Life may seem comfortable, and you don't want to mess up a good thing. However, if life is merely a series of efforts to avoid messiness—to avoid heartache, unease, and suffering—it is a sad, hollow life indeed.

Is my life messier with Lucy? Is it harder? Well, yes. She chatters constantly and is emotionally unpredictable. She can appear the picture of security one week and then cling to me for dear life the next. Vacations have been shelved; finances are tighter. Life was definitely easier pre-Lucy.

But, oh, our days are richer. When her chubby hand reaches for my face, strokes my cheek and says, "I love you, Mama. And you love me," when she leaps around the living room, hand-in-hand with her sister as they do their special "sisters' dance," when she discovers something new every single day, when her once blank face is now full of emotion, when her very presence teaches us new and deeper truths about God's redeeming love . . . we just know.

Adoption is a gift that wrecks your life
in the very best way.

We wouldn't go back to those "easier" days for all the money in the world, not only because we couldn't imagine our lives without our sweet girl but also because Jesus calls us to a much greater purpose in life than the easiest route available. Our utmost calling is to reflect His glory to an unbelieving world, and this calling often requires hardship. But it's the kind of hardship that reaps far greater rewards than this life could ever give.

Father,
Thank You for the incredible calling You give me through Christ. You want so much more for me than what my idols—comfort and ease—seem to offer. Thank You for the amazing privilege of living out this calling through adoption. I pray that the world will watch and see my joy as I invest in the eternal rather than the temporary. I pray others will be encouraged to step out in faith instead of clinging to a false sense of safety. Thank You for loving me enough to wreck my ordered life—I wouldn't have it any other way.

Day 8

WHEN GOD SAYS "NO"

All the days ordained for me were written in your book before one of them came to be.

—Psalm 139:16

*I*t was early in our adoption process, about nine months down the road. We decided early on to let our agency match us with a child instead of us pursuing a particular child from the waiting list. Even though this was the plan, I still scrolled through the list of waiting children every time our agency sent out an email with these sweet faces. If you felt the Lord speak to your heart about one of these little ones, you could request to see the file and investigate further.

It was through this casual scrolling that she caught my eye: a precious two-year-old, tiny and frail, who had a heart condition.

I stopped scrolling, fixated on this petite little face. I couldn't look away.

Is it you? Could you be the one?

We requested her file and were given a week to decide if we wanted to submit a Letter of Intent, the official document to the Chinese government saying we would like to be this child's forever family. We sought counsel from a pediatrician who specializes in international adoption; we prayed and agonized and prayed some more.

Brian and I both knew: the answer was no. This child was not to be ours.

That email was so difficult to write. How could we say no to a little girl who desperately needed medical care and a mama to rock her to sleep and whisper words of love and life and forever? How could God tell us to say no?

One of the most painful risks of adoption is the loss of a child who was never fully yours. Birth mothers sometimes change their minds at the last minute. Referrals are not always approved. Countries may suddenly close their doors, making a child no longer adoptable. And then, like us, perhaps you are the one who for some reason has to say no to a particular child. This decision hurts terribly, and the pain is deep.

When you lose a child through the adoption process, the grief is intensely real. You may have already named this child. You might have set up a beautiful room in your house. Your heart was deeply invested, and now it's shattered into tiny pieces that feel like they will never be put back together again.

My goodness, this hurts.

But for the Sovereignty of God, where else would we go?

God has written a great narrative, and it doesn't just include your story; it is also the story of the child who is no longer yours. And the story of the little one who *will* one day be yours. Do you trust Him as the author of the overarching tale, even when it deviates from your original plan? Do you trust that while you can only see in part, He sees the whole, and the whole is good? Do you trust Him with your pain, your disappointment, and your grief?

"The LORD is close to the brokenhearted and saves those who are crushed in spirit" (Psalm 34:18) the Psalmist declares. He is, and He does. I know firsthand.

Another family I know received a referral of a tiny little girl and prayed over her beautiful picture. They agonized and went back and forth but somehow knew that she was not their daughter. God said no, so they did too. It was one of the hardest things they'd ever done, but they continued to pray for this little girl, that God would not delay in bringing her forever family to her and that she'd soon be home safe and sound.

Imagine their surprise when they saw a post on their agency's Facebook group, announcing China's official approval of another family's application for that same little girl! They just had to make contact with this family they'd been praying for. So, they sent this message:

....

We wanted to let you know we have been praying for your family and your daughter. We were given this file to review and chose to pass on it. It was a really difficult decision, and we have been praying for her and her forever family. We are so happy for your family and can't believe we are on the same Facebook group and with the same agency! Small world. We are so relieved to know she has a family. . . . We will continue to pray until you can get that sweet girl home.

....

The child's name? Lian Yonghui, who became Lucy Mei. Our Lucy.

God's *no* to another family was His *yes* to us, and His yes to Lucy, and to the little girl who eventually became this family's daughter—the one He had waiting for them all along.

Dear friend, His plan is and always has been perfect and good, even though we don't always have eyes to see. Let this be our comfort and our hope when we are drowning in the pain of the nos.

> ## Father,
> I know that You desire to give me good gifts. Just as a father wouldn't give his son a stone when he asks him for bread (Luke 11:11), I know that You don't withhold good things from Your children. But it sure feels like sometimes You do. Would You give me the courage and faith to trust You when You say no to my heart's desire? Please comfort me as only a Father can, and then gently remind me that You are trustworthy and in control. Help me to trust You, the author of not only my story, but of the Story—the greatest story ever written—the rescue plan for broken souls. I only see in part, but You see the whole. I can't wait to one day see the fullness of Your masterpiece in that place where grief and disappointment no longer exist. What a great day that will be!

Day 9

A MIRACULOUS MOMENT

God sets the lonely in families.

—Psalm 68:6

*A*ll the waiting. The paperwork. The worry. The imagining of what he will look like, or what it will feel like to hold her. The doubting: "Are we doing the right thing?" The nerves. The obsessive email checking. It all culminates in one event—*The Day.* Adoption Day.

You've rehearsed this moment in your head over and over. Will you reach for her or let her come to you? Should you and your spouse embrace him at the same time, or will that be too much? You've played out every possible scenario. You've changed your outfit fifty-six times. Your stomach is in knots. You want time to hurry up and slow down, all at the same time. You're ready. *What if you're not ready?*

The moment finally arrives. Perhaps you received a middle-of-the-night phone call, and you're at the hospital about to hold her newborn warmth in your arms. Maybe you received travel approval just days before, and you're sitting in a Civil Affairs Building in an unfamiliar land. Maybe you're pacing the halls of your house, listening for the social worker's car, and you hope your new son likes his room you redecorated twelve times to get it just right. *"What if he doesn't even like trucks? I should have gone with a sports theme!"*

Then, when your heart can't possibly take another moment's delay, there he is. There she is.

Quiet—listen now, do you hear it? Peel back the curtain into the heavenly realm, and you just might hear a faint din of celebration. As an adoptive Father Himself, God must be delighted in that moment, *the* moment, when an orphan is placed in his parents' arms for the first time and is transformed into a son . . . when a little girl whose future was so uncertain is at last a daughter. Walls of nationality and background and baggage are torn down. A new story has been written; a family is made whole.

At the moment of adoption, a supernatural transformation occurs in the tender hearts of parent and child, even if they don't feel it immediately. Sometimes the connection is instantaneous for all parties—and what a relief that is!—but not always. My Lucy?

She cried. She leaned as far away from us as she could possibly get. We looked funny, sounded funny, and we were too close for comfort for a child who had spent most of her young life in isolation.

No, feelings of affection on either side are not always immediate. Do you know what? It doesn't matter. Not one bit. The fact is, no matter how that first meeting goes, at the moment of adoption, you are standing on blessed ground.

Just think about it! Think of all God accomplished to get you and your child to this sacred event. God planted in your heart the desire to adopt. He conquered fears and doubts, deadlines and financial inadequacies. He overcame your own feelings of inadequacy. He said, "Keep going! Just a little while longer. You're almost there!" All the while, He was preparing a child for you, causing your stories to intersect at just the right time. He knew exactly when you would become a family for good, and that moment has finally arrived.

Theory has become reality.

It is one thing to dream about adoption; it's another thing entirely to stare lovingly into a stranger's wary eyes and gently declare, "Yes, I will be your mother. Would you please allow me the privilege of being your mother?" Only God could orchestrate such a moment, and it is simply magnificent.

Despite what that instant was like or will be like for you—no matter if there is laughter or embracing or awkwardness or rejection or grief—know that something stunning has happened in the spiritual world.

> *Forget the former things; do not dwell on the past.*
> *See, I am doing a new thing! Now it springs up;*
> *do you not perceive it? I am making a way in the*
> *wilderness and streams in the wasteland.*
> *—Isaiah 43:18–19*

God is in the business of making things new. He specializes in making beauty from ashes and reclaiming the years that brokenness has stolen. He loves to forge a trail of safety when the terrain feels wild and treacherous. On Adoption Day—The Day—He makes a way once again, and He rejoices. He rejoices in your obedience, He rejoices in a life made new, and He rejoices to see His adopting heart reflected in your own.

Father,

You love to make things new. Only You could conquer countless obstacles to deliver my child safely to me in Your perfect timing. What a holy moment! When the days are long, will You draw my eyes to this moment? Remind me, Father, of Your faithfulness to my child and to me. It is only by the power of Your transforming grace that such an unbelievable moment could ever come to be. Thank You, once again, for transforming me at the instant of my adoption as Your child. There is no better family for me than Yours. I praise You for making me new then and every day since.

Day 10

BIRTH MOTHERS— OUR HEROES

Honor one another above yourselves.

—Romans 12:10

*I*f you had a chance to talk to your child's birth mother, what would you say?

If you're like me, words would fail you. How could you sum up the gratitude, the respect, the feelings of inadequacy that well up when you meditate on the enormous gift a stranger has entrusted you with? Could you really communicate the humble reverence you feel toward her decision to give your child life, to make the ultimate sacrifice so that your little one could have a future? Could she know how much you have prayed for her—how much you've thanked God for her courage and begged Him to comfort her in her pain?

Perhaps if you wrote her a letter, it would sound something like this note I wrote to Lucy's birth mom, a woman I'll never have the privilege of meeting or even mailing this letter to. As you read these deepest stirrings of my heart, I pray you are moved to worship and to praise God for the woman who gave your child the gift of life.

To Lucy's birth mother,

I'm thinking about you a lot these days.

I wonder what you look like, how you spend your days. I wonder if you're married and if you have a child underfoot at home. Are you serious or lighthearted? Daring or withdrawn?

I wonder what life was like for you that mid-September day, not too long ago.

Abandonment is a harsh word; yet harsh is not how I would describe the scene that is painted in my head of how that day went for you. Perhaps a better word is anguish or maybe desperation. Definitely pain.

Just days after giving birth, you must have been exhausted—filled with sorrowful dread as you anticipated what you felt you must do. Although I'll never know the circumstances surrounding why you did what you did, I believe that you bravely chose the best chance at life for your daughter.

I play out the possible scenarios of that day all the time. I wonder: When you laid her in that place where she would be easily found, did you run away before you were seen? Or like so many in your same situation, did you slip into the shadows, watching to make sure she was carried to safety before you turned—empty-handed—for home?

Home, I imagine, has never been the same since.

I cannot fathom the agony, and I am so sorry for the position you were forced into. I am so very sorry for your pain.

I wish there were a way to let you know that she has a home now, that your desires for your little one's life are being fulfilled. Even though I desperately long for circumstances and laws to be different so that she could have remained yours, I am so thankful God called my family to be family for her.

Oh, how I wish you could see her now! Just shy of five months being ours, she is transformed. She started out as a kid who was scared of food, and now we can't feed her enough! She loves anything—zucchini, sweet potatoes, bananas, and pears—but regretfully, I have to say her favorite is cake. And who can blame her? I wonder: do you have a sweet tooth too?

She lights up the room with her silly grin and infectious laugh. She loves games like peek-a-boo and tickle monster, and really anything that causes us to give her our undivided attention. She loves to read (usually the same book again and again) and the more animal sounds the better. She says, "Baa!" when she spots a sheep, and "Neigh!" when she discovers her friend, Mr. Horse. She is a smart little thing.

She has two brothers and a sister who think she hung the moon. They don't even mind when she cries. She has a daddy who would lay down his life for her. When he leaves for work in the mornings she shouts, "Bye-bye Da-Da!" and it's all he can do not to stay.

She lays her head on my shoulder when she's sleepy, and shouts "More! Please!" when she sees food. Her favorite bath toy is a teapot, and she giggles with delight when her big sister pours water over her head. She likes to sleep on her tummy with her ducky blanket spread across her, and her favorite bedtime song is Andrew Peterson's "Beautiful Girl," "Hey, beautiful girl, [Mommy] loves you, [she] loves you, most beautiful girl in the whole wide world." We end our bedtime routine with that one every night.

I know hearing some of these things might be painful for you, yet I'm sure you would want to know that she is so deeply loved. I want you to know I do not take being her mother lightly because I understand that you had to relinquish the title of "Mama" in order for it to be my own. This name was given to me at great cost to you, and, oh, how I want to make you proud.

I promise to love her tenderly, protect her fiercely, and provide for her every need and desire as God enables. And I promise to talk about you every chance we get so she knows that not just one but two mothers have loved her well.

We honor you, even though we'll never know your name. Lucy may not be in your arms, but you are and forever will be in her every smile, laugh, pensive gaze, and sheepish grin. You chose to give her life, and you are a part of her. I am so very grateful.

Behind each beautiful adopted child's face is a mother who embraced life when she could have easily chosen otherwise. Let's honor her as God's precious creation—the bravest woman we've never known.

Father,

You were there when a certain woman found out she was pregnant. You held her hand as she agonized over what to do. You embraced her in those final moments when she said that excruciating good-bye, and You grieve with her when she feels the ache of longing for what couldn't be. Thank You that You have not left her alone, Father. Love her well, this woman who gave me the greatest gift I'll ever receive. I pray she'll understand that You too said good-bye to Your only Son for the sake of love. I pray that she'll find peace, hope, and security in a relationship with You. Hold her close, Lord, and provide for her every need until hopefully she and I will meet in heaven and embrace as two mothers who loved our child the best we knew how.

Day 11

ADOPTION IS NOT NATURAL

Let us not become weary in doing good,
for at the proper time we will reap a harvest
if we do not give up.

—Galatians 6:9

*W*hen my husband and I had our first biological child, we felt completely ill-equipped. I'll never forget the day we were being discharged from the hospital after our oldest was born. The nurse quickly ran through some tips for our baby's care, and then she said we were free to go.

Wait. That's it? Aren't there any more instructions? Where's the manual? You're not just going to let us leave, are you? We felt absolutely clueless and incapable. Although we were overjoyed, we stumbled about exhausted, flustered, and shell-shocked. It took us forever to do seemingly simple tasks like dressing him and buckling him into his car seat. With the addition of a tiny child, two competent adults became awkward novices.

This same sort of awkwardness occurs between parents and adopted children, but at a whole new level. In this relationship, both parties start out as strangers, without the advantage of bonding in utero. Even if a child is adopted at birth, the voice of his adoptive mother is different from the voice he heard for the first nine months of his life. And for parents who adopt older kids? There's a lot of lost ground to make up; affection and connection must be earned. This process can feel clumsy as parents and child try to figure each other out.

If you think about it, adoption is not natural at all. We all want the beautiful family photo featuring a well-adjusted child and happy parents, but this picture takes time to create. Parenting a child born to someone else is not God's original, natural design, but it is part of His redemption.

It's a little bit like the process of sanctification, isn't it? Perfect obedience and unhindered relationship was God's original design, yet the introduction of sin into the world made this no longer possible. But God, in His great love, had an elaborate rescue plan to redeem and restore what had been broken. His Son Jesus was the chosen change agent, whose offer of hope and new life would make relationship possible once more.

So, we respond in faith to His salvation call, but we're not immediately comfortable in our new skin. The Christian life holds an element of awkwardness as our flesh rebels against what the Spirit says is right and good. There is struggle and rebellion and doubt; we feel clumsy as we try to figure out what God requires and what holiness is all about.

What then do we do? We persevere in obedience. We continue to pursue relationship with the One who never stops pursuing us. The more we choose obedience, the more obedience becomes the easier choice. The more natural it actually feels.

In our first days with Lucy, I was clumsy. I bought her the wrong size clothes, and I didn't know how to put her to sleep or what soothed her when she was upset. I didn't know her favorite games or what signals she gave when she was overly tired. I irritated her because I got too close, and I upset her when I was too far away. And now? A few years down the road, I know that when she says, "I'm not sleepy, Mama," it means she needs her bed pronto. I've memorized the way her squishy hand feels in mine, and I automatically reach down to her exact height when she's beside me with her ready palm. I've memorized the streaks of chestnut that appear in her hair when the light hits her head just so, and I know that bubbles always make her laugh. I know that when she lays her duck blanket over her fist and rubs it on her nose, she will be asleep within five minutes. I know that when she cuts her eyes and smiles a big, wide grin, she's been up to some kind of mischief.

Our relationship wasn't natural at first, but with each passing day, with each exchange of trust and love as we dive deeper into knowing each other and being known, it is more so. And as we obey our Father, we become more familiar with His heart, and His desires become our own. Sin and righteousness gradually switch places—sin becomes what's awkward and uncomfortable, and righteousness feels like home.

Feeling awkward in your relationship with your child? Press on. Keep loving, keep pursuing, keep laying a foundation of trust and familiarity, one day at a time. Eventually, your relationship just might feel so normal that you'll question how you ever did life before this child came along.

Feeling clumsy in your relationship with Christ? Keep obeying, even when you don't feel like it. Even when your flesh tries to persuade you toward a seemingly "better" way. Feed the spirit, and you'll reap the fruit of the spirit. And one day you'll realize that it feels like you've known the Father all along.

> Father,
> Sometimes I feel clumsy in my relationship with my child. There's so much to learn, so much ground to cover, so much lost time and affection to make up for. Help me to persevere as I look forward to the day when we're at ease with each other. And God, sometimes my relationship with You feels awkward and forced. Sometimes I don't want to obey, and it seems much easier and more natural to go my own way. Help me to stick with obedience; help me to feed my spirit instead of my flesh, trusting that one day it will be more natural to follow You than not. Thank You for the joy that parenting and obedience bring.

Day 12

LIVING WITH LOSS

Not only so, but we ourselves, who have the firstfruits of the Spirit, groan inwardly as we wait eagerly for our adoption to sonship, the redemption of our bodies.

—Romans 8:23

*W*hile we seek to honor our children's birth mothers, there is a reality of loss that cannot be avoided. I feel it most with one spoken word, and it happens every time it's uttered. Without fail.

There is a title I worked months to earn, that I waited years to hear articulated. From the time I knew we would gain a daughter from across the ocean, I prayed about it, pleaded for it, and then tried to lay down a foundation of security so that I might hear it spoken out loud, by her. What did I want so desperately to be called by my tiny beauty?

Mama.

I knew I was her mama, but to hear that word loft from her lips as a sweet offering of acceptance and intimacy—it would be the culmination of so many dreams and prayers.

She spoke it for the first time about three months after her Adoption Day, mouth awkwardly maneuvering into position, trying to find her voice. Then at last: "Mmmaaammmaa."

I was prepared for the joy, the elation, the relief I experienced with that sweet spoken word. *At last! She knows I'm Mama.* Do you know what I wasn't ready for? The grief. Even now, when she looks at me with eyes full of trust and love that have been earned over many months, leans in close and stage whispers (because she can't quite whisper softly yet), "You're my mama," my heart contracts. It contracts with so much love and gratitude for the place to which we've come that I'm overwhelmed. Yet simultaneously . . . at the same exact moment . . . it squeezes with grief for the woman who originally bore that name. Right or wrong, my heart can't help but whisper, "She should be saying this to her," and I want to weep for this woman. I don't at all feel guilty for being Lucy's mother, but I ache because of the brokenness that made it necessary for me to be her mother.

The heartbreaking part of adoption is that in a perfect world, it would not exist. Families would stay together. Mothers would not be forced to leave their little ones behind. And so, we live in a constant state of dichotomy. With every milestone achieved, with each new display of affection or familiarity, we celebrate—and we mourn. We mourn for the one who would not, who could not remain in this priceless role of mother.

As our kids get older, they feel it too. No matter what age a child is when adopted, there may always be an underlying sense of grief. Even infants adopted at birth can carry around a subconscious burden of loss that, in most cases, will somehow surface throughout life. They know they are special, they know they are chosen, they know they are loved, but they also know their stories were birthed out of brokenness, and it hurts.

How do we—and our children—live with loss in a way that is redemptive instead of debilitating?

Disney attempted to answer this question in the surprisingly profound hit movie, *Inside Out.* The main characters of the film are the emotions of a little girl named Riley: Joy, Sadness, Fear, Anger, and Disgust. While trying to navigate a season of loss in Riley's life, Joy realizes that Sadness is a crucial component of Riley's emotional health. If Sadness is not recognized and embraced, Joy is superficial and forced.

How true this is! If we simply stuff, hide, or ignore the very real element of loss in our children's stories, the joy we try to offer them will feel shallow. If we choose not to recognize our own hearts' opposing contractions of happiness and sorrow as we grow in intimacy with our children, we will never fully appreciate the gifts that have sacrificially been given to us. To be human is to experience both emotions simultaneously and not deny either one access to our hearts.

So, we celebrate milestones. We cheer on bonding and trust, and then we weep for the very same things. We weep for our children. We weep with our children. We say, "I know this isn't how it's supposed to be. I'm so sorry."

But there is more.

Disney did well, but they did not paint the full picture. As believers we know that this dichotomy will not always exist. There is a King who will return to make all things right, a Savior who will absorb the sorrow. In this we have amazing hope, and we can offer this hope to our children. Through tears we can proclaim, *"Dear ones, this is not how it will always be.* The King is coming. The King is coming! One day, the light will dawn and remain. The ache will dissipate. You will no longer feel conflicted. You won't have to feel happy and sad for the exact same reasons. You will only find it easy to love. The day is coming—just you wait and see."

And then? Joy. Only joy.

> ## Father,
> My soul is groaning. Creation is groaning under the weight of brokenness that will not fully heal until You come. My heart is breaking over the history of my little one, and sometimes I don't quite know what to do with my child's pain or my own. Thank You for allowing me to be an eyewitness to Your redemptive work in my child's life, and thank You even more that You are coming to make it right again. Until then, Lord, help me to fully embrace the joy and sorrow that coexist, knowing that I can experience You equally in seemingly contradicting emotions. Come quickly, Lord Jesus. I long for You to make everything right again.

Day 13

PATIENT PURSUIT

*But God demonstrates his own love for us
in this: while we were still sinners,
Christ died for us.*

—Romans 5:8

I'm not sure what I was expecting. I'd read the books and completed extensive online training on trauma, attachment, and bonding. I knew there was a good chance Lucy wouldn't warm up to us right away. I knew that for our new daughter, meeting us would seem more like an alien abduction than a feel-good Hallmark movie, but for some reason, I just wasn't prepared.

I wasn't ready for the rejection.

I longed for a soft embrace; I was not prepared for rigid, stick-like arms to rise in self-protection. I desired nearness; reality was a terrified child who leaned as far back as she possibly could, not daring to risk contact. I envisioned a happy, whole family; instead, I received stares at the hotel restaurant in Guangzhou as little Lucy screamed and refused to eat, leaving the other five of us feeling stressed and overwhelmed.

We would have died for her, but she did not want us. Could anything be more heartbreaking?

See, a biological child is naturally bonded to his or her mother at birth because her voice has been known for months already. A biological mother does not usually have to work consciously to earn her child's love: most of the time it is simply given. Not so for adopted children. They are asked to embrace complete strangers, and the prospect can be terrifying. This terror can often manifest as rejection of all things new, including their family and home. These little ones don't know what they need so they resort to what they already know—isolation, fear, and survival.

Sound familiar? It should, because we too can distance ourselves from our Father who knows exactly what we need.

"I made you!" God says. "I fashioned you intricately and know even the number of hairs on your head. I know exactly what your soul needs to thrive, and it has nothing to do with those imitations you're chasing after. Will you trust Me? Will you allow Me to meet your needs?"

"But this all looks strange and unfamiliar, God. I've never been where You want to take me, so how can I know that it's good? My plans are working out for me pretty well. My friends Comfort and Entertainment and Self-Fulfillment are meeting my needs just fine, thank you. I think I'll stick with them."

"Those idols will not satisfy; I will. I created you and I love you," He answers.

We lean back. We avert our gazes. We stiffen at His approach and tense at His touch. If we could just go somewhere . . . anywhere other than here . . . *If He would just leave us alone!*

"I love you," He calmly repeats as He takes a step toward us. "Even though you don't want Me, I died for you. I paid the greatest price when you didn't even know who I was—when you had no idea I was coming for you—and I would do it again."

"But I'm afraid."

"Perfect love drives out all fear, dear one, and I'm the only One who loves you perfectly. I will pursue you until you believe My love and your walls come down. I'm not going anywhere."

His love is a patient pursuit.

Lucy's arms eventually came down. Little by little, her defenses fell away, and persistent love won. We didn't give up on her, and praise God, He doesn't give up on us either, despite our stubbornness and fear.

We can rest in these promises concerning His faithfulness to pursue us to the end:

The Lord is compassionate and gracious, slow to anger, abounding in love. —Psalm 103:8

If we are faithless, he remains faithful, for he cannot disown himself. —2 Timothy 2:13

The Lord is not slow in keeping his promise, as some understand slowness. Instead he is patient with you, not wanting anyone to perish, but everyone to come to repentance. —2 Peter 3:9

When we're discouraged by our children's hesitancy to reciprocate our affection, we can look to Christ's wonderful, ongoing example of what it looks like to pursue loved ones in the face of rejection. While we were still sinners—when we did not want Him—He gave His Son for us. When we wander again and again, He gently loves us back into relationship. He does not tire of our weakness; He is a kind and long-suffering Friend.

Father,

I can be so slow to believe that You are what's best for me. It's sometimes difficult for me to believe that You know what I need even before I do. Forgive me for running; forgive my disbelief. Thank You for Your enduring patience. Thank You for wooing me back to Yourself with Your perfect, faithful love. Help me to lower my defenses and trust You as my Maker, Redeemer, and Friend. In the same way, help me to pursue my child with love and grace. When my child pushes me away in fear and rejection, give me Your eyes and Your compassion—especially when I'm tempted to give up. Remind me again and again that love is patient, even as I am a grateful recipient of Your own perfect, long-suffering love.

Day 14

LONELINESS

Praise be to the God and Father of our Lord
Jesus Christ, the Father of compassion
and the God of all comfort, who comforts us
in all our troubles, so that we can comfort
those in any trouble with the comfort
we ourselves receive from God.

—2 Corinthians 1:3–4

*I*t happened over coffee. Our family was in the application portion of the adoption process, up to our eyelids in paperwork, and I had asked a seasoned adoptive mom to meet me at a cafe so I could learn from her experience, pick her brain about potential pitfalls in the adoption process, and maybe get a little encouragement to keep filling out all those forms. In the course of our conversation, she shared about a particular struggle between her adopted and biological children. Because I have three biological kids who seem to argue constantly, I thought I could relate.

"Yeah," I replied, "but all kids say that about their siblings at some point, don't they?" Something unreadable flashed in her eyes, and then she graciously conceded, "Yes, they do." The conversation moved on.

I didn't understand my ignorant blunder then, but now I do. There was no way the sibling tension in her home was the same as my kids' arguments because our family dynamics were completely different. In an effort to relate, I probably made this woman feel more misunderstood.

Isolation is a common theme for adoptive parents because we can feel as if no one understands us. Well-meaning friends think they can relate to our children's struggles with eating, sleeping, bonding, school, and a host of other things, but they really can't—not completely. Loved ones try to empathize, but their comments can miss the mark and feel dismissive.

Here's what a few adoptive parents said they wish others understood about their lives and their children:

> *"I wish they understood that I love my adopted children as much as they love their biological ones."*

> *"I wish they understood that we are still the same people. Having adopted children doesn't mean we no longer like or do the things we did with our biological children prior to adoption. We want friendship and support more now, not less."*

"I wish they understood it hurts when someone asks questions about our children compared to 'normal' children."

"I wish they understood that we aren't adopting because we just have to have more children! I've heard people say, 'Well don't you have enough already?' But what they don't understand is that it's not about having enough. It's about answering God's call to care for the fatherless and love our neighbor. It's about love for God and for others."

"I wish that they understood that our family is different from their families."

"I wish people knew that when they tell us how awesome we are or how they could never do what we do, it takes away our ability to say how hard it is."

"I'm a single mom to two Chinese princesses, and sometimes I feel like I have to keep my thoughts and struggles to myself because I've had comments made to me about how I chose to be a single parent to two. Actually, the Lord chose me. I never dreamed I'd be a single parent once, let alone twice."

"I wish people realized we don't need answers or advice; we just need a listening ear, a text, a phone call, a meal, or a coffee date—something to help us feel connected to the out-side world when those first few weeks and months home are hard. And sometimes the years are hard, and we need people to understand that we are the same but different. God took us on this journey of adoption, and that 'yes' has changed us in many ways. We have new opinions, goals, and priorities. We may forget to call or text you back. We may parent our children differently now, and some of that looks weird. We need grace and understanding as we navigate this new world we ventured into."

Often one of the worst forms of suffering is being misunderstood. It hurts, and it's lonely. Thankfully, we have a Savior who is well-versed in compassion toward our situation because He is possibly the most misunderstood person in history. He loves to express His empathy through the comfort He so readily gives, and He is eager to bear our burdens for us.

But Jesus doesn't give us comfort just so we'll keep it for ourselves; He comforts us so that we can in turn comfort others. Has the Lord encouraged you when you've felt that others just don't understand? Find a friend who is also struggling, and share your newfound inspiration with her. Did God meet you in your loneliness? Seek out the lonely, and offer companionship and understanding. Has the Lord drawn you out of isolation through His loving, patient pursuit? Pursue others with the same loving-kindness, even if they don't seem to respond right away.

While we crave understanding and empathy from others, we won't get it—not perfectly, not every time we need it. But God sees. God knows. God comforts with the gentlest of care. And by His grace, on the toughest of days, His compassion is enough.

Father,
It is so painful to be misunderstood. It's not easy to feel different from others, and I long for empathy from those around me. But no one can know me perfectly, and no one can love me perfectly except for You. I run to You, God, as my source of comfort, understanding, and care. As I receive my portion of Your compassion, let me not just keep it for myself, but help me to be quick to share that compassion with others. The only reason I can even hope to care for others well is because You first reached out to me, so thank You for providing a perfect example of unconditional, forbearing, never-failing love.

Day 15

WORTH IT

If a man owns a hundred sheep,
and one of them wanders away, will he not leave
the ninety-nine on the hills and go
to look for the one that wandered off?

—Matthew 18:12

*Y*ou and I make choices every day based on the value of things. We assess the worth of opportunities clamoring for our time, of products that claim to be worth our money, of the endless to-dos that demand a piece of our energy. We subconsciously have conversations with ourselves all the time that sound something like this:

> *"Such-and-such product is on sale at X store, but it's a 20 minute drive away. Nah, I don't think it's worth it."*

> *"If I wake up early to go the gym, I'll only get five hours of sleep, and I'll be cranky all day.*
> *It would be better for me to get some extra rest."*

> *"My favorite artist is performing the concert of a lifetime in my hometown. I don't care what tickets cost—*
> *I'm going. It will absolutely be worth every penny."*

In our economy of time, energy, and resources, there is careful examination of pros and cons, of what return we'll get on our investment. If a choice doesn't work to our advantage or benefit us somehow, our natural inclination is to decline. We may not admit this cost analysis approach out loud, but if we're honest with ourselves, this is how we often operate.

God's economy is way different.

Jesus made some seemingly crazy choices of how He spent His time and energy. He invested the greatest portion of His resources into twelve ordinary, thickheaded men who had a tendency to bolt at the slightest hint of trouble (John 18:15–18). He dined with the underlings—the folks with whom no one wished to associate—instead of positioning Himself with people of greater power and influence (Matthew 9:10–12). He criticized the leaders we would think He'd have wanted on His side should things get dicey, and He praised those who held the lowest social positions (Matthew 23:1–36). He invited scandal into His life by associating with women and by making what would seem to be blasphemous claims like, "I'm God" (John 4:7–26; 8:58). He challenged those who wanted a high position in His kingdom by telling them to become like children if they really desired greatness (Matthew 18:3–4).

Jesus also told some confusing stories, at least to our understanding. He talked about seeds that sometimes grew and sometimes didn't (Matthew 13:1–10). He compared a rich man to a camel (Matthew 19:24).

He spoke of a shepherd who left his safe, healthy flock of ninety-nine to search for one measly, directionally challenged sheep (Matthew 18:12–13).

Who would do that? Who would put a sure thing at risk to save something so small and seemingly insignificant? Who would, according to Jesus, gain more happiness over the rescue of that one lost sheep than the fact that the ninety-nine stayed?

The Great Shepherd, that's who. The One who gave up everything to rescue you and me.

God had an amazing, redemptive plan. He made the decision to leave glory and pursue a people who had nothing to offer Him in return—a people who would mock, accuse, doubt, and reject Him . . . who would choose Him and then quickly forget His goodness at the first signs of trouble . . . who would taste His love and then give in to fear, and then run to Him again.

It's Jesus' example of love at all costs that gives us courage to pursue our children in the same manner. We need as much bravery as we can get because we all experience moments of, "Is this worth it?"

"This process takes forever! Is it really worth it?"

"We're stretched so thin financially. Is it worth it?"

*"She may not even like us. He may resent us one day.
Is it worth it?"*

"I'm just so tired. Is it worth it?"

God's economy says "Yes." Worth the time, worth the financial sacrifice, worth the sleepless nights, worth the wrecking of your ordered life, worth the potential for rejection. No matter how your child receives love, it is always worth it to give him your love. No matter how she responds to affection, it is always worth it to lavish your affection. No matter how good or bad your day is as a parent, that lamb—that one sheep that is wandering through the devastation of abandonment—is worth throwing all caution to the wind. That child is worth the cost of leaving behind what is sure and secure so he can be brought home—for good.

God loved us and declared us worthy of the most treacherous pursuit. Because of His great love, because of His selfless sacrifice in the face of potential rejection, we can choose faith and declare under the most difficult of circumstances, "Yes, my child is worth it."

Father,

You love me with such an extraordinary love. You saw me wandering, lost and alone, and You sent Your Son to be my Great Shepherd. I had nothing to give You, yet You sacrificed all You had to give me what I needed most: relationship with You. Thank You for valuing me so much that You enacted the most daring rescue plan in history. God, let Your sacrifice give me courage to pursue my child at great cost and sometimes peril, to always believe that he is worth it. That she is worth it. When I'm discouraged and want to throw in the towel, help me to look to the patient, tender love You extended to me when I offered You nothing. Help me to remember that in Your economy, it's far better to give than to receive. Let my willingness to give not be contingent upon what I'll get in return.

Day 16

NEW FAMILY, NEW NORMAL

For whoever wants to save their life
will lose it, but whoever loses their life
for me will find it.

—Matthew 16:25

*O*ne of the major factors in our adoption decision was whether or not our kids were on board. After all, we were asking something pretty big of them. At this point in time, we had a smooth life rhythm as a family of five. What did the kids think about making space for one more? How would they feel about us disrupting their sense of normalcy? We especially wanted to hear from our little girl because we felt our decision to adopt would affect her the most. She had not only been the lone daughter but also the youngest child for a good six years. Was she willing to be dethroned?

All three kids were in with an immediate "Yes." Sarah Kate danced around the room, shouting, "I'm going to be a big sister! I'm going to be a big sister!" The boys were thrilled too.

Yet theory is one thing; reality is another. Theory says, "This is going to be awesome!" And there are definitely remarkable moments. My daughter got the sister she always dreamed of, and she has delighted in her role as big sis from day one. She loves playing with Lucy and teaching her new things. The boys adore their baby sister and love to show her off to their friends.

But there's another side to reality. While there are extraordinary times for the kids as they dote on their Princess Lucy, reality also reveals their heart cries of, "This does not always feel so awesome."

Reality for families trying to blend biological and adoptive siblings can look like a drastic change in family dynamics. For us, it meant we were back to baby days and naps and, "Be quiet, you'll wake your sister!" It meant no longer being able to do some of the things our family loves to do because it would be too much for Lucy. Reality is a child forced to grapple with jealousy when Mom is now doting over someone new. Reality is sharing space in Dad's lap. Reality is stressful after-school hours when the noise and chaos are too overwhelming for a sensory-sensitive one, so tears are the norm. Reality is Mom swinging baby back into a calm state out on the front porch instead of assisting with homework or music, instead of being readily available to play.

When we choose adoption, the whole family sacrifices; everyone is affected. It may seem as though our families lose their identities, and this is not easy by any means. But I wonder . . . could that loss actually be a good thing?

According to Jesus, when we lose, we actually win by a landslide.

"What?" you ask. "How can that even be possible? Who in his right mind likes to lose?"

Jesus said if we want to protect our lives, if we only desire to keep our lives safe, neat, and tidy without risk or sacrifice, then we will actually end up losing our lives. This truth extends to our families as well. If our main goal in parenting is to protect our children—to stand as a force field between anything that threatens their happiness or potential for success—then we are setting them up for disastrous failure.

Thank goodness Jesus gave us another option.

He said if we will lose our lives for Him—if we will pry open our hands and lay down our neat little plans, if we will take our children outside of our overly protective bubbles and allow them to follow Jesus' example of entering into humanity with empathy and sleeves rolled up ready to do kingdom work—then we will gain, for ourselves and for them, the best kind of life there is: a surrendered life. A life that makes a difference in this world and the next.

Maybe my biological kids had to slow down their pace of life when their sister came to town. Maybe they lost some of my undivided attention. Maybe I can't volunteer as readily for school field trips, and maybe I've missed a few soccer games. Maybe they've lost sleep because their sister sometimes cries in terror in the middle of the night. But what have they gained in return?

Selfishness has been exposed and repented of. Egocentric tendencies are being turned outward as compassion blooms. Rigidity is constantly forced to bend for the good of another. Their eyes have been opened to the suffering around the globe. Their desires to be entertained and made happy are being transformed into longings to make a difference in this broken world.

While not easy, the new normal is a gift for everyone. A life lost for Jesus is infinitely better and richer than the protected life we think we need. Children with empathetic eyes open to the needs of those around them are what we truly desire, more so than kids who are self-centered and unaware. Let's stop looking back to what was and instead, with grateful hearts, embrace the gift of family life being shaken up for good.

Father,

You've given me a desire to protect my children, and this is a good thing. But fear and selfish motivations twist that God-given desire. I am often guilty of idolatry as I worship my kids' safety and happiness. Thank You for the new normal You have given me through adoption. The ripple effect of my chosen one's arrival into my family's tidy life brings blessings richer than I could have ever imagined—blessings like the transformation of my biological children's hearts. Thank You for the softness I see—for their newfound compassion and increased burden for the world around them. Help me to always choose a surrendered life over a merely safe life.

Day 17

LEAN IN

Come to me, all you who are weary
and burdened, and I will give you rest.

—Matthew 11:28

I used to take pictures of my kids in my head. Before the days of social media, before our obsession with capturing and posting life online every minute of every day, I would catch magical moments and click my internal camera, willing myself to never forget the image before me. I had such a moment one day when my oldest son was in kindergarten. He walked out of the school as the day ended, spotted me in the sea of waiting moms, yelled, "Mommy!" and then sprinted, arms wide open, into mine. I thought, "There will come a day when it's not so cool to run into Mom's arms with your friends looking on. Remember this moment, Jennifer. It will not last."

The reason why I didn't want my son's unashamed affection for me to end was because it was a natural part of our relationship. There had never been a day that he didn't fit just right in my arms, when he didn't want my embrace. It would be such a loss for him to outgrow the need for my arms.

Fast forward ten years, and I found myself longing for the affection of a child who refused to give it, who simply did not know how. A child who fought my touch with rigidity, who flung herself backwards when I tried to hold her close, even at bedtime. With my oldest son, his affection was mine to lose; with my newly adopted daughter, I feared her love would never be mine to gain.

Is it possible that we reject God's affection in a similar way?

We all do it at some point because we don't always love the story He writes for us. We may demand a plot revision, a change of characters, a better ending. Maybe it's the waiting we don't like. Maybe it's the unexpected degree of hardship our adoption journey has brought with it. Maybe we hate the surprise twist of conflict in a story that was supposed to lead to happily ever after.

When we're disappointed with the story, we can become resentful of the author. So we stiffen. We lean back. We fight against His embrace and demand to be left alone. We try to punish Him with our silence as if He doesn't already know our most private thoughts. Our hearts rebel, and we don't even want to be near Him.

But what if we took a different approach? Instead of fighting Him because of our burdens, what if we accepted His invitation to lay our burdens at His feet? What if we took Him up on His invitation and actually *came to Him*? If we could accept the story He writes for us—even though some parts seem scary, uncertain, or downright unfair—and then leaned in, we could actually rest. Really rest. We could have that deep soul's rest that each of us crave but rarely pursue, if only we would lean in. After all, leaning in, not out, is the natural posture of a parent and child.

Lucy did finally lean in. On a night that began like many others with bath time and pajamas and stories, I started to rock my sweet girl, facing her away from me, the way she always preferred. Then I wondered, "Should I just try it?" I turned her toward me and slowly began the rhythm of back and forth, back and forth as I sang, "Jesus loves me, this I know . . ." Her unyielding body pushed away from mine like usual, but something told me to persevere. The longer I sang, the heavier her eyes became. And then, with caution at first, and then with newfound trust, Lucy laid her head on my shoulder for the first time ever, and drifted into a safe, contented sleep.

Victory! Lucy finally did what a child was made to do—rest in her mother's embrace. She fit just right, as if she'd been there all along. It was where she was meant to be.

What is your posture before the Lord? Is it stiff, with hands up as you lean back as far as you can go? Are you refusing to accept His plan for you? Are you unwilling to receive His affection and care? Or are you leaning in—relaxed, surrendered, and at rest in the arms of the One who made you, loves you, and who lovingly wrote your story from beginning to end? Lean in. The comfort we're looking for is not in answers or changed circumstances or in an easier child; it is in His embrace. Cease fighting, friend. He is calling you to lean toward Him and rest.

Father,

Your arms are always open wide. Thank You for giving me a standing invitation to come to You, lay my troubles at Your feet, and rest. Forgive me for rejecting what's best for me, for blaming You when things get hard, and for then withdrawing from relationship with You. Help me to lean in, even when it's awkward, even when I'm angry or sad or fearful. When I stiffen and move away from You, remind me that Your embrace is the best and most natural place for me to be.

Day 18

THE BURDEN
OF GUILT

*But when he saw the wind,
he was afraid and, beginning to sink,
cried out, "Lord, save me!"*

—Matthew 14:30

*M*y adoption agency has an entire staff dedicated to postadoption support for families. As in, there are people on call, ready to help with any range of issues, from cocooning to attachment to caring for the mental health of their adoptive parents. In their pre-placement training, the staff emphasizes, "Call us. If you say you're not struggling in some way after your child comes home, then we know you're not telling the truth."

I was given permission to admit that postadoption life is challenging. I was told I would experience difficulties, that I could voice my struggles, and that I would be well cared for when I asked for help.

Do you want to know how many times I've made that phone call? Once? Twice? A half dozen times? Actually, none. Zero. And it's not because our agency was wrong about the challenges they predicted and, actually, life is bliss. It's not. So what's holding me back? What's holding you back from saying, "This is really hard!" and then seeking assistance from those who are ready and willing to care for you?

Guilt.

Here's the problem: When a biological mother gives birth to a child, people expect her to feel overwhelmed. Everyone knows that she is a mess physically, mentally, and emotionally, and it will take time before she adjusts to her new normal. We get this, so we give her lots of grace and urge her to do the same for herself.

Yet for some reason, we adoptive parents sometimes feel guilty about struggling with our own adjustments. We may assume that if we share our struggles, we will be judged because this path is what we chose, right? We filled out the forms. We raised the necessary money through countless fundraisers. We chronicled our journeys to our children on our blogs. We said, "I know this road will be difficult at times, but my child is worth it, no matter what." So we think we're not allowed to struggle, at least publicly. We may be drowning, but we think we can't tell anyone because adoption is supposed to always be happy and beautiful—never mind the fact that no parent-child relationship is ever happy and beautiful all the time.

Peter knew what it's like to step out in faith and then quickly realize you're in over your head. He and his buddies were out to sea, waiting on Jesus to finish His prayertime on the mountain. The night was uneventful until Jesus came out of the dark fog, walking on top of the very water they were floating on. Everyone was terrified, thinking it must be a ghost. Yet Peter (in his typical fashion) asked Jesus to call him out of the boat and onto the water, so he could see if Jesus really was who He said He was. Jesus did as He was asked, and in a giant leap of faith, Peter climbed out of the boat and placed one tentative foot, and then another, onto the sea. Amazingly, his footing held, and he was on his way to the Savior. All was well until Peter took his eyes off of his teacher and looked at his surroundings. The wind had picked up, and the waves looked menacing. Peter immediately began to sink (Matthew 14:22–30).

Now, imagine if Peter's thought process went like this as the breakers crashed over his head: "I'm the one who stepped out of the boat! The boys are all looking to me as an example of fearless faith. I can't ask for help—attempting to walk on the water in the middle of the night was my decision, so I just need to power through this storm. No one needs to know I'm struggling."

Poor Peter. This self-sufficient talk would have gotten him drowned for sure. Thankfully, he did the exact right thing: He hollered out, "Lord, save me!" and he didn't care who heard him. He knew his situation was dire, so he called to the One who could rescue him from a watery grave. Jesus helped Peter back in the boat, their relationship intact. He may have exhorted Peter to keep his eyes on Him, but Jesus didn't shame Peter for falling.

Don't be ashamed to admit that adoption is sometimes hard. Look how quickly Jesus came to Peter on the sea when he cried out for help! He came immediately. If you are in a hard season, name your pain with freedom, believing that Jesus will hear you and come quickly to your aid.

When you confess your weakness, you'll bless others in the process as well. Look how the disciples responded to Peter's declaration of weakness and rescue: *They worshiped.* They got to witness their Savior respond to Peter's cry and pull him from the brink of death, and they were awestruck. "Truly you are the Son of God," they spoke, with eyes wide and jaws dropped in utter amazement (Matthew 14:33). Don't cry out to the Lord alone; bring the body into your mess. You'll heal as your brothers and sisters in Christ love on you, and you'll minister to them too. Perhaps your own vulnerability in hardship—your willingness to admit weakness and cry out to your Savior without caring who sees you—will grab the attention of those around you and leave them awestruck at the Messiah's immediate, tender care.

> Father,
>
> Your Word says it is for freedom that You have set me free (Galatians 5:1). Your death on the Cross means no more guilt or shame; my debt is paid in full. Because I am free, help me to walk in authenticity and vulnerability with others when I hit bumps along the road as a parent. Forgive me for trying to parent out of my own strength and for not letting others, or You, in on my struggles. Forgive me for being too proud and afraid to ask for help. I sometimes forget that I was never meant to walk this road alone. Remind me to honestly cry out to You and to reach out to others when I am drowning. I know that the resources You are ready to provide through Your Word and the body are abundant, so thank You for Your provision. I entrust my burdens to You.

Day 19

THE BEST VERSION OF YOURSELF

*Just as the Son of Man did not come
to be served, but to serve, and to give his life
as a ransom for many.*

—Matthew 20:28

*I*t had been five years since Brian and I had been away on a trip for more than just a night or two. Lucy had finally gotten to a stage where she would be comfortable with us leaving her overnight, so we took the plunge and planned our fifteenth anniversary trip to Melbourne, Australia, and the Great Ocean Road.

The best thing about this trip of a lifetime was not the breathtaking scenery, although it was exquisite. No, the main reason why this vacation was amazing was the fact that for an entire week, we were responsible for no one but ourselves. We slept in every morning, ate lunch at 2:00 p.m., dined at restaurants that had no kids' menus, and explored the city on foot for eight hours straight at our own pace without factoring in extra bathroom breaks or rest stops that little legs frequently need.

I could have stayed there forever. No deadlines, no demands, no conflict.

And then . . .

We arrived home on a Friday night, refreshed and recharged, and within 24 hours, all four kids and Brian had the flu. As in the real deal, I-want-to-die flu. They dropped like flies, one by one, right before my eyes:

"I'm cold."
"I don't want any dessert."
"Can I go to bed?"

Back to life, back to reality . . .

In a matter of hours, we went from complete serenity to germy chaos and my flesh screamed, "I want to go back! I want to go back to beauty and peace and freedom from responsibility! Take me back to the impossibly blue skies and turquoise water and what I feel is the very best version of myself. I mean, *really*. I was happy! I was carefree! I wasn't irritable or tired or stressed, and isn't that a good thing? *Let me go back.*"

Do you ever find yourself wanting to retreat? Do you look at the mess around you—the stress of the adoption process, the child who is crippled by fear even though you've given every ounce of energy and attention to making her feel loved and secure, the days with your child that feel like two steps forward and three steps back—and you just want to run away and disengage, if only for a little while? It would be so much easier, wouldn't it?

If you're like me, you identify with Lucy in *Prince Caspian*, who saw the battle raging all around her but had no desire to fight. She only wanted to remain at Aslan's side—away from the danger, away from the uncertainty.

Perhaps this sounds like you:

"Can't I just skip the battle? Can't I sit out the moody teen years and the illnesses that strike families down in a single blow and the fight to love when I'm not loved in return and the battle for my child's affections and security and the daily struggle to slay my selfish heart? Can't I just curl up next to Aslan's side to rest and simply be? Can I please go back to the holiday at the sea? It feels safe there. There's no conflict there. I don't lose my temper there. It's easy to love there."

But vacation is not reality. There will be a day for perfection and eternal peace. The time will come when for all eternity we can sit by our Maker and enjoy the warmth of His presence and light, and there will be no reason to fight because the war will have already been won. But for now, the battle rages on—in our own hearts, in our imperfect families, in the ache of all humanity who want to know what it means to be truly seen, known, and loved. Right now, we're called not to simply bide our time until the trumpet sounds but to engage redemptively with fighting siblings and a messy house and sulky preteens and dear chosen children who still feel insecure sometimes, and may always feel so.

Heaven is coming, but for now, there is kingdom work at hand.

So, we wipe another fevered forehead. We serve another bowl of soup. We repent of our selfishness and love that little one who needs more from us than we feel we have to give, trusting God to provide the extra energy and grace. We marvel at how our souls are renewed when we take our eyes off ourselves and serve, at how it really is true that "whoever refreshes others will be refreshed" (Proverbs 11:25).

Yes, heaven will come. It will. Until then, the best version of our self is not Vacation Self, but Servant Self with hands dirty, knee-deep in humanity, daily choosing to engage in the mess.

Father,

So often my flesh wants to escape the trials of this life. I look around me, and it all feels like too much—the needs around me are just too great, and I feel like I have nothing left to give. Will You refuel me, Lord? Will You help me to look to You for my strength when I just don't want to persevere, when I want to disengage and chase after what is easy? As I draw strength from You, help me to joyfully and willingly serve those You've entrusted to me, knowing that I'm never more like You than when my hands are dirty from engaging in the mess of humanity.

Day 20

TRUST EQUALS FREEDOM

*I have come that they may have life,
and have it to the full.*

—John 10:10

*O*ne of the greatest joys of adoption is watching trust evolve right before your eyes. For some families, this happens quickly, maybe even right away. For others, it takes time—trial, error, and oftentimes tears—for this transition to occur. I had a front-row seat to this evolution each week at the park, of all places. Pretty soon after Lucy came home, she and I joined a playgroup with some families from our church. For months, Lucy only sat in my lap and observed warily. She wasn't very mobile at that point, but it was obvious that she felt unsettled as she silently clung to me each week. We never stayed for very long, and it wasn't much fun for either of us. As she got steadier on her feet and a little more comfortable with her surroundings, she started to climb on the playground equipment, but only if I was right beside her. Months passed, and she played a bit more independently, allowing for some space between us. But she never interacted with the other kids. I secretly thought, "Is she ever going to actually play with anyone other than her family?" I really didn't know the answer.

Still, we persevered. After more than a year of play dates at the park, it finally happened. I lost sight of Lucy for a second and scanned the park in a moment of panic. Imagine my surprise when I saw her playing *with* other children! Tentatively at first, and then with a little bit more confidence, she joined right in with the fun. She played chase and "hide in the tunnel" and make-believe ice cream shop. She laughed and jumped and sprinted back and forth across the playground, giggling toddlers at her side. I had to practically drag her sweaty, dirty-faced self to the car after two hours of hard play. She didn't want to leave her new friends. Friends! She actually called them friends!

What finally clicked? What changed a clingy, fearful child into a boisterous playmate? Trust begat freedom. We had finally reached a level of trust that no longer required me to stay constantly at her side. She believed that I wasn't going anywhere. Because she trusted, Lucy was free to enjoy the beauty of her surroundings; she was free to accept offers of companionship. A timid morning at the park transformed into an imaginary world shared by friends, and this version of playgroup was a lot more fun.

Greater trust equals greater freedom, always. For all of us.

What elements of abundant life do we miss out on because of fear? What relationships do we needlessly throw away, or never begin in the first place, because we're afraid? Jesus promised to not only give us life but life to the fullest—a bubbling, overflowing kind of life that is much more fulfilling than mere survival. But our enemy Fear loves to show up and steal our joy by taunting us with words like *rejection*, *failure*, and *defeat*. He is so convincing, isn't he? This enemy is the culprit behind so many abandoned dreams, friendships, and adventures.

What if we slammed the door in Fear's face and instead threw down the welcome mat and opened the gates of our hearts to the One who says, "Trust Me"?

*We would experience true community because we would be
freed up to initiate with others from a place of security.*

*We would pursue dreams that we've shelved
for "the right time."*

*We would be fully present instead of trying to recreate the
past or being paralyzed by the future.*

*We would try lots of new things because we wouldn't worry
about looking foolish to others.*

*We would stop assuming the thoughts and motivations of
others and instead believe the best.*

*We would know and feel known as we open our fragile
hearts to others and they unlock theirs in return.*

The list could go on and on. When we trust the One who is before all things and holds all things together (Colossians 1:17), we are freed up to not just experience life, but experience it to the full.

Before our family moved overseas, a friend advised, "Life on the missions field is like a high-speed roller coaster. You can either grip the rails, holding on for dear life, or you can throw your hands up and enjoy the ride." Life in general is like this, isn't it? You can grit your teeth, dread every bump, and anticipate the big drop with your eyes clamped shut, or you can open your eyes and see the beauty that's around you. Either way, you're going to get to your destination, so you might as well enjoy the view as someone who is free. Even better? Enjoy the view with others.

"It is for freedom that Christ has set us free" (Galatians 5:1). Because Jesus has changed us, we are free to love Him with reckless abandon, and we are safe as we fail along the way. Let's live out the freedom that we've already been given through salvation, trusting our Maker with every tiny detail of our lives.

Greater trust. Greater freedom. Life more abundant.

Father,

You are so trustworthy. You have proven Yourself over and over again, yet when I look around at my circumstances, when I give in to fear, I forget that I've been set free. I miss out on so much when I don't trust You. Remind me, Lord. Remind me of how much better life is when I operate out of the freedom You've given me through Your Son. You've already granted me abundant life, so help me to choose to walk in it, saying no to fear and yes to trust.

Day 21

MAMA ALWAYS COMES BACK

*And surely I am with you always,
to the very end of the age.*

—Matthew 28:20

*S*ecurity is something we all long for, isn't it? Even though God offers eternal security through a relationship with His Son, even though we experience the freedom that comes from resting in our adoption into His family, we still doubt Him from time to time. We wonder if He'll really always be there. We question if it's really true that He'll never leave us alone.

We learn so much about this dynamic from watching our kids struggle to rest in the security we offer them as their forever parents. We may prove a hundred times over that we are trustworthy, that we aren't going anywhere, and we may witness progress and victories like Lucy had at the park, and yet insecurity can flare up at any time without warning. The need for security may always be a prominent theme, even for a child who was adopted at birth.

It took a year and a half for Lucy to walk into her Sunday School class tear-free. We celebrated this day like it was Christmas.

"She didn't cry! We both got to hear the sermon! She was easy for her teachers!" We thought this day would never come. Corner turned; we've done it. Happy at church? Check.

But then a few weeks later, I was summoned out of the service because Lucy was in hysterics—as in big, gulping breaths, red-faced, nose-running, I-cannot-recover kind of crying. What in the world? I thought we had conquered this milestone! Why didn't she feel secure? I snuggled her, spoke truth to her about how much I loved her and would never leave her, and was baffled—if not a little discouraged—by her meltdown. Later that day she brought up the event.

"Why did I cry in my class?" Lucy asked.

"I'm not sure. Why did you cry, Lucy?" I gently responded.

"Because I wanted you," she whispered, her dark eyes wide as they searched mine for reassurance.

"Oh, Lucy, I wanted you too." I held her close. Then, an epiphany. Lucy brightened.

"But Mama always comes back," she declared. "And I'm safe."

What a holy revelation! Lucy may have momentarily questioned her safety, but the truth of my unconditional love returned to her, and she could rest in the certainty of her status as my child, a role that will never, ever change.

We can experience this same kind of holy moment with God. Unlike me, He is never surprised when we doubt His love. He knows that we are limited by our humanity. The fact is, we are simply incapable of trusting perfectly all the time.

God is very familiar with this scene: Uncertainty clouds our perspective, fear sets in, and we cry out, "Where are You? Where did You go? Are You coming back?" We become unsettled, then panicked. Our thoughts follow our fears down the rabbit hole of irrationality, and pretty soon we're questioning if He loves us at all. Yet we must believe in the depths of our hearts that He actually is near because we call to Him and expect an answer.

"Where are You?"

No, He is not surprised. He responds with the utmost care.

"I'm here. Why did you cry?"

"I wanted You," we whisper, wondering if He'll be disappointed by our fear.

"Yes, I want you too," He assures. "But I'm always here. I will never, ever leave you. You are safe. *You're safe.*"

And then we remember His promises, and we recall the precedence He set by never failing us in the past.

"Oh, that's right . . ." we sigh, as our insecurities fade with each recollection of His acts of love and faithfulness.

We remember these promises:

Never will I leave you; never will I forsake you.
—Hebrews 13:5

For I am the LORD your God who takes hold of your right hand and says to you, Do not fear; I will help you. —Isaiah 41:13

99

*Surely God is my salvation; I will trust and not be afraid. The L*ORD*, the L*ORD *himself, is my strength and my defense; He has become my salvation.*
—Isaiah 12:2

When we let the truth of these verses wash over us, a sense of calm returns. "Yes, Lord, You are always here and I can rest in You." Anxiety subsides, and we can taste sweet peace once again.

Will we ever trust perfectly while on this side of heaven? No. But perhaps the next time we're shaken, our recovery time will be quicker, or maybe the next time life throws us a curveball, we'll be a little slower to take our eyes off Him. As our security grows, hopefully our initial response to trials will be more faith and less fear. And when we are afraid, we can be sure that He'll be right beside us to speak words of truth once again.

Mama may always come back, but God never leaves, not even for a few minutes.

Father,
Thank You for reassuring me again and again that You will never leave. I am so prone to wander. I am prone to doubt Your commitment to me even though Your faithfulness to me has been flawless. Thank You for Your patience and loving-kindness that woo me back to You every single time I give in to fear. Thank You for being a perfect Father who never leaves, no matter what.

Day 22

THE COMPARISON TRAP

Lord, you alone are my portion and my cup; you make my lot secure. The boundary lines have fallen for me in pleasant places; surely I have a delightful inheritance.

—Psalm 16:5–6

*M*y eight-year-old daughter is obsessed with a particular brand of stuffed animals that have big, sparkly eyes, cute names stamped on their heart-shaped tags, and birthdays that demand to be celebrated. Each time she adds one to her collection, she's giddy with delight. She's perfectly content with the stuffed animals she has until she hears of someone having more. A friend might bring a stuffed fox in for show-and-tell, and suddenly she can't live without that fox. She goes to someone's house to play, and the first thing she reports when I pick her up is how many of these toys that friend has and how much she wants those particular animals too. Heaven help us if we step foot in a toy store. If you're eight and a mound of big-eyed, adorable animals is staring you in the face, pleading with you to make them your own, your collection of a dozen or so suddenly seems measly in comparison.

Comparison. That's the word. It's as much of a temptation at eight years old as it is at thirty-eight. And sixty-eight. I'm content with my house until I visit someone with a nicer house. I'm fine with my wardrobe until I stroll through the mall. When I gaze a little too long at the grass that seems so much greener on the other side, I'm no longer content with my plot of land.

Each one of us is guilty of comparison. No one is immune.

The comparison trap began in the Garden when Eve listened to the deceiver as he spoke of what she didn't have, of what she *should* have. Even though God had given Eve and her husband literal perfection and complete access to Himself, Eve bought the lie that it wasn't enough. The seed of discontentment took root in her heart, and her lot in life no longer seemed pleasant. She ate what was not meant for her, what was not hers to take, and the world has never been the same since (Genesis 3:1–7).

When are you enticed to glance around? When are you tempted to look over the shoulder of the Provider as He holds His perfect provision, take inventory of what others have, and compare that list to your situation? I believe this temptation is great within adoption communities, and social media isn't helping us out one bit. We obsessively check our agency's social media page to see how our waiting times compare with others, to make sure our cocooning practices are up to par, to see how our children's development compares with other similar-aged kids. Are we behind in the bonding process? Should we be seeing more specialists? Look how this other child is speaking so clearly! *Something must be wrong with my child.*

Comparison only breeds pride or discontentment, every single time. Either you're puffed up because you feel like your child, your parenting, or your situation is superior, or you're miserable because it seems others have it better than you do. You think, *Their child is easier. Their adoption process is smoother. Their attachment with their little one is quicker and stronger.* You conclude that you obviously do not measure up.

Without fail, comparison robs us of our joy.

Yet, God Himself has assigned us our portion, and it is good. It may seem at times that others' portions are much bigger than our own, but He has given us exactly what we need.

When we stop looking around, we are freed up to celebrate the blessings right in front of us. When we truly believe that our portion is good, pride and insecurity fall away, and we can be fully present in the life we've been given instead of fretting because it looks different than what others have received. We can delight in our children and marvel at their bravery; we can celebrate their progress without measuring it against some imaginary timeline that we're convinced they must match.

And you know what else? We can enjoy each other. God created us for community. From the beginning He knew it wasn't good for us to be alone, and that's been our story ever since. We need the body. Period. We thrive when we have others around us walking our paths with us, fighting to love and obey right alongside us. We function best with the love and support of others. Don't let your pride or insecurity isolate you—community is way better than comparison any day of the week.

If godliness with contentment is great gain (1 Timothy 6:6), then let's pursue the holy character of Christ with the contented attitude of Christ—humble, dependent, and thankful—and look forward to the rich blessings that will then be sown in our lives and the lives of those around us.

> Father,
>
> I fall so easily into the comparison trap. From the beginning I've been influenced by the enemy who says that what I have is not enough. Forgive me for not believing that what You've given me is right and good, for thinking that Your provision is not the perfect portion for me. Give me eyes only for You and Your plan for me, and help me to celebrate with others instead of wishing their victories for myself. Thank You for the rich blessings that You've lavished on me—the ones that are right before my eyes, and the ones that I can't even see yet. Thank You for the gift of community.

Day 23

ADOPTION CAN ROCK YOUR MARRIAGE

Be completely humble and gentle; be patient,
bearing with one another in love.

—Ephesians 4:2

*O*ur daughter had been home about six months. Our family was gathered around the dinner table, all six of us miraculously in the same place at the same time. The older three were taking turns talking—and talking over each other—as they relayed the highlights of their days. Lucy's loud, incessant chatter drowned them out—an endless droning of nonsensical words and melodies that was her brain's way of coping with the barrage of sensory input coming at her. I softly sang nursery rhymes to her, the only way to calm her down and get her to eat, all while trying to affirm my kids' stories with the occasional, appropriately timed "Uh-huh . . . oh, wow . . . that's great." Above all of this noise, the only interaction my husband and I had at the table was snappy comments and looks that screamed, "I am losing my mind, and you'd better do something about it."

Adoption is hard on your marriage.

No one wants to talk about this, and not much is written on the subject, but it's true. How could it not be? A child enters your family in an unnatural manner. Love and attachment are not immediate; they take time to grow. If your child has special needs, this is an added challenge that demands constant extra attention and care. If there are other siblings in the family, guilt over neglecting their needs to care for their brother or sister hangs heavy over both parents. If adoption follows infertility, the depth of the pain from that heartbreaking road can continue to spill over into marriage for a long time to come.

So what do you do? How do you thrive in your marriage under such potential stress? You definitely want to prepare for the pressure beforehand by talking through the potential stressors. It's also crucial to put safeguards in place such as getting others to pray for you and prioritizing quality time, even if it's just connecting over a bowl of ice cream after the kids are asleep. But do you want to know the very best thing you can do for your marriage?

Run to God's Word.

Thankfully, the Bible's commands for how we should treat each other don't come with disclaimers such as, "This only works during low-stress seasons of life." Actually, Scripture holds true even in—*especially in*—the most difficult of times. This is what God says about how we can love each other well:

Serve One Another (Galatians 5:13)

When you feel like you cannot do one more thing for another human being, serve your spouse, even if it's in a small way. Encourage her to go for a jog while you watch the kids. Buy his favorite kind of junk food. Fold the six baskets of laundry even though you're desperate for your bed. Offer the largest brownie. The smallest act of kindness goes a long way to encourage a weary heart.

Be Devoted to One Another in Love (Romans 12:10)

When you see your spouse at their very worst, affirm your commitment to them through your words and actions. They don't need someone to tell them what they're doing wrong or how their attitude is less than holy; they already know. Be a safe place for the other to fall when they crash in a heap of exhaustion, regret, and despair. Show that you love them in spite of their shortcomings, and remind them that you're not going anywhere.

Choose Humility, Gentleness, and Patience as You Bear with One Another (Ephesians 4:2)

Overlook offenses and choose to believe the best. Humility begets humility, so humble yourself and respond with gentleness and patience, even if you're not the one who is in the wrong. There is great wisdom in the proverb, "A gentle answer turns away wrath, but a harsh word stirs up anger" (Proverbs 15:1). Choose gentleness when you want to retaliate, and you may be surprised at how quickly the tension is defused. Patiently champion the Jesus you know is in your spouse even when the fruit of the Spirit isn't easily seen. They may have temporarily forgotten their identity in Christ, so tenderly remind them that they are a dearly loved child of the King.

Forgive Each Other (Colossians 3:13)
Forgive much because you've been forgiven much.

Apologize to Each Other (James 5:16)
There is such freedom in humbly saying, "I was wrong. Please forgive me."

Pray for Each Other (James 5:16)
This is the best thing you can do for your spouse. Adoption is one of the most challenging roads there is, so bathe your spouse in prayer, in order to strengthen and encourage them as they fight sin and try to choose love each day.

Encourage One Another (1 Thessalonians 5:11)
You can be the greatest source of encouragement for your spouse. Your words hold more weight than anyone else's, so be the first one to praise and the last one to criticize.

We won't follow these commands perfectly, but we can make them our aim, praying God will give us the strength of character to consider the other better than ourselves—even when all we really want after hours of pouring ourselves out, day after day, is to be served. Only the Son of Man, who deserved to be served but came to serve instead (Matthew 20:28), can transform our hearts so that we are able to serve in the same way.

Our marriages can actually deepen and thrive under the stress of adoption if we will be honest about our struggles, overlook offenses and, with humility, choose kindness. Walking the journey together as allies instead of enemies will help us achieve what we each want: a secure, loving home built on the solid foundation of Christ.

Father,

Thank You for creating marriage. It is such a gift through the joys and struggles of life, even though I don't always recognize it as a gift. Adoption is not easy on my marriage, and the enemy knows that. It's so tempting to give in to selfishness, to claim rights, and to feel like I deserve to be treated a certain way because I'm sacrificing so much to care for my children. Thank You for providing the example of Jesus who came to serve, not to be served. Help me to follow His example even when I'm exhausted and have nothing left to give. Protect me, Father; make my marriage strong, especially on the most stressful of days. The best way I can love my children is to love my spouse well, so help me to do just that.

Day 24

WHAT IF I FAIL MY CHILD?

But he said to me,
"My grace is sufficient for you,
for my power is made perfect in weakness."

—2 Corinthians 12:9

*I*t's an impossible age in which to be a parent. Thanks to our easy access to any and all information, we are bombarded daily with messages of how to parent successfully and how to fail miserably. "Feed them this, but not that!" "Affirm them, but not too much!" "Discipline consistently, but make sure they feel heard and understood." "Attachment parenting is best, but make sure you raise them to be independent." You could read one hundred blogs a day and discover one hundred different ways to be a stellar parent who never lets their kid down.

Add to this pressure the complication of raising a child with special needs (and some would argue that all adopted kids have special needs because of their traumatic start), and the expectations are crippling. Because of the complicated nature of our children's backgrounds and the fragility of the bonding process, parenting mistakes feel more costly. As a result, we find ourselves parenting with the mantra, "There is no room for error."

This pressure to be faultless is misconceived and debilitating because the truth is, we will fail our children. We don't want to, but we will. We will make obvious mistakes that we will immediately wish we could take back, and we will make mistakes without even being aware we've made them.

Do you trust Christ to fill in the gaps these mistakes create, especially the ones that you don't even know exist? Because can I tell you something? If Christ can't cover both our blatant and unintentional parental folly, then we are absolutely sunk.

When we mess up, the enemy—always the opportunist—jumps in to shame and accuse:

"See? I knew you would fail!"

"The only thing to do is try harder.
You must double up on your efforts. Read more books.
Buckle down on intentional time."

"You must fix this."

Oh, no. Satan is a liar and a thief, and we need to tell him so when he throws these accusations in our faces. Yes we will fail, but isn't that why Christ came? Because we can't be perfect? We can't perfectly parent "easy" kids, and we can't perfectly parent challenging kids with extra needs. Thankfully, God has given us an answer for the enemy's accusations: "Therefore, there is now no condemnation for those who are in Christ Jesus" (Romans 8:1). God says, "Look around. Who is actually able to accuse you? Who now has the authority to shame you? No one. *No one.*"

Do we want to be intentional with our children? Do we want to do everything we can to love them well and provide a secure base for all things in life? Yes. But if it is up to us to make sure that nothing goes wrong in their lives, then we may as well jump ship right now because it simply isn't possible.

There is grace for that.

We will not parent perfectly, but praise God, He will. Thankfully, our children have a much greater Advocate who will fill in the gaps that our shortcomings and plain old humanity will inevitably leave. In and of ourselves, we are not enough, but God is.

I SAY . . .

> *The dishes need washing, the baby needs holding,*
> *And I am not enough.*

> *Tears need drying, praise needs to be given,*
> *And I am not enough.*

> *Conflict needs resolving, fears need soothing,*
> *And I am not enough.*

> *Dinner needs cooking, trauma needs healing, habits need*
> *replacing, security needs enforcing,*
> *And I am not enough.*

BUT GOD SAYS . . .

I am here; I have what you need.
I am enough.

What your child requires, I can give.
I am enough.

You are completely free in grace.
I am enough.

You will fail, but that's why I came.
I am enough.

Father,

You are enough. That declaration is so freeing when I choose to not only believe it but to walk in it as well. Thank You that although I don't have all the resources necessary to love and parent my child well all of the time, You do. Thank You for filling in the gaps that my humanity leaves. I know that Your grace is sufficient for me. It is when I'm at my weakest that Your power is on its greatest display, so I thank You for my weaknesses. I trust You as the only perfect parent, and I choose to rest in Your finished work on the Cross for me.

Day 25

GOD,
DO YOU SEE ME?

*She gave this name to the L*ORD
who spoke to her:
"You are the God who sees me."

—Genesis 16:13

*E*verything should have gone as planned. I had quadru-ple-checked to make sure we had done everything according to the required procedure. We could not get this wrong; too much was riding on us doing things right.

Sure, adopting a Chinese girl through the American adoption system while we were living in Australia was a tad complicated, but hundreds of expats had gone before us and done the same thing. Our agency was seasoned in this very complication, so everything was going to be just fine.

Except it wasn't.

Lucy and I flew to America immediately after her adoption to secure her United States citizenship and obtain her passport. After obtaining these precious documents, we would then fly back home to Australia, where my husband Brian and our other three young children were waiting. In an unbelievable turn of events, Lucy's passport application was denied . . . and then her US citizenship was denied.

We weren't going anywhere. My new daughter and I were stuck half a globe away from the rest of our family, and no one knew what to do.

One of the most painful aspects of my fight for faith during this dark time was feeling ignored by a God who was supposed to love me. I constantly asked, "God, do You see me? Either You don't see me, or You are simply indifferent."

Have you been there? Have you felt ignored or overlooked by a God who is supposed to work all things for your good and His glory? Have you felt forgotten by Him as you walk down a path He told you to take?

Maybe your wait for a child feels endless.

"When will we be chosen? God, do You see me?"

Perhaps you've gotten so very close, only to get that agonizing phone call: "The birth mother has changed her mind . . ."

"God, You must not see me. If You saw me, You would know there is no way I can handle this kind of agony. If You saw me, You wouldn't have let this happen."

Maybe your child has rejected you or is acting out in ways that seem to be destroying your family. Your child's traumatic past may feel insurmountable.

"God, where are You? *Do You not see me?*"

A woman named Hagar asked this very same question. Hagar was handed a rough lot in life. Ordered to sleep with her master Abraham, she became pregnant with his child—a son Abraham and Sarah were too impatient to wait for God to provide. The affair was actually his wife Sarah's outrageous idea, but when the plan was executed, Sarah became bitterly jealous. She couldn't even stand the sight of her servant, so she mistreated Hagar until she eventually ran away. What else could Hagar do? (See Genesis 16:1–6.)

This poor woman. Pregnant by another woman's husband without any say in the matter, abused, forced to flee her home, hiding in fear, utterly alone.

Until God met her in the desert.

God came to Hagar and spoke directly to her. He let her share her hurts, and then He promised that her story was not over yet.

Can you even imagine Hagar's response? The God of the universe stepped down from heaven to enter into her suffering, to be with her in her pain. She was so overwhelmed that she gave God a name—El Roi, the "God who sees."

I can hear her now:

"You see me. *You really do see me.* You see me in my heartache and panic and rejection, and because You've come close, I can now see You."

Not only did Hagar feel seen by God, but in being seen she saw Him too.

"I have now seen the One who sees me" (Genesis 16:13).

This too can be our story.

Dear friend, His name is El Roi. "The God who sees me" *sees you too.* It's not just that He sees all things in the universal sense, but He specifically, intimately sees you in your pain and desperation. He sees every tear cried late at night when the house is still and the nursery is empty, every word spoken in frustration, every argument with your spouse, every ache you feel when your child refuses to accept you as home. He sees. He loves. He is there.

Let the reality of His knowing, loving gaze turn your eyes to Him so that you see Him too. As He sees you in your weakness, look to His strength. As He enters into your brokenness, stare into His perfection. As He looks with compassion at your battle scars, don't miss the fact that He has them too—wounds borne on your behalf so that you could one day be made whole.

It's no coincidence that God met Hagar at a well. It's in our desperation, in our hours of aching loneliness and affliction, that God invites us to drink deeply of living water from the well that will never run dry (John 7:38).

He's waiting for you at the well today. Do you see Him? He surely sees you, and He understands. Go to Him and drink.

> ## Father,
> Sometimes I feel so alone in my suffering. It's easier to assume that You've abandoned me than to believe You could allow my pain and still be good. But You haven't left me, and You never will. Thank You for being the God who sees—who doesn't just see all of creation in a general sense but actually sees and knows me. Lift my head so that I can see You too and be refreshed.

Day 26

DO I HAVE A DESERVING HEART?

But Martha was distracted
by all the preparations that had to be made.
She came to him and asked, "Lord, don't you care
that my sister has left me to do all the work
by myself? Tell her to help me!"

—Luke 10:40

*I*t was the home stretch. We were weeks away from leaving everyone and everything we knew and loved. We were following through with our crazy plan to move to the other side of the world. Emotions were high, simmering just below the surface and spilling over at the slightest provocation. We were drowning in logistics as we tried to conquer our never-ending to-do list while wrangling three children and trying to spend precious time with loved ones. We felt as if our lives were in utter upheaval, and we were desperate for help, compassion, and care. The closer we got to the departure date, the more needy we felt, and the more sensitive we became to how others related to us. Too often, Brian and I found ourselves unfairly criticizing the actions of our loved ones.

Even though our friends and family truly were loving us well, we had thoughts like, "Why won't they help us more? Don't they care that we're walking through the hardest days of our lives thus far?"

We sought counsel from a wise friend who had a discerning take on our reactions. He said, "Be careful: the degree to which you feel you are sacrificing can be the degree to which you feel entitled."

Yikes. Rebuke received.

Here was the reality of our hearts: "We are moving to the other side of the world! We're giving up everything, so you should sacrifice too! Nothing in your life could possibly be as important right now as helping us."

Entitlement. Martyrdom. "You owe me, because look at the sacrifice I'm making."

Pretty ugly, huh?

I would have never expected the same demanding spirit I struggled with when we were moving overseas years ago to rear its ugly head in our adoption journey, but it did. It still does.

Has entitlement ever crept up in your heart? Do you feel it there now? Adoption is a sacrifice in so many ways—financially, emotionally, and physically. It stretches us beyond our limits, and emotions can become raw, threatening to bubble over at any moment. If we're not careful, we can harbor resentment toward loved ones who we feel should sympathize with us or help us more. We may become extra sensitive toward what we feel others are *not* doing for us.

"This is so hard! Can't they see I'm drowning here? Why don't they check on me more than they do? Why can't they understand?"

Mary's sister Martha can relate. Jesus, *the Messiah*, was coming to eat at her house. He was actually coming! There was so much to be done—food to prepare, floors to sweep—the list was endless! Oh, no. He's here and things aren't ready yet. Martha knows she will have to miss some time with Him because lunch won't cook itself. Hustle-bustle, hurry-scurry. Martha wipes her sweaty brow with her apron and tells herself to just keep moving.

What's this? Mary is nowhere to be found! Where could she be? There's so much to do! Oh, no. No she didn't. She's in there with Him? Must be nice! That's exactly where Martha wants to be, but she can't—not with the dishes piled high in the sink. She marches over to Jesus, her honored guest, and demands that He instruct Mary to help her. She's been slaving for hours—surely she deserves some help!

But Jesus doesn't scold Mary; He encourages her. He praises her choice of presence, and exhorts Martha to follow suit.

> *"Martha, Martha," the Lord answered, "you are worried and upset about many things, but few things are needed—or indeed only one. Mary has chosen what is better, and it will not be taken from her." —Luke 10:41–42*

What is the better choice for you when your degree of sacrifice tempts you to demand help, affirmation, or validation from others? In layman's terms, "Put the broom down, Martha." Not that you must stop serving altogether—it's kind of impossible because you can't simply stop being a parent—but slow down long enough to think about your motivation for serving. Is the way you view your sacrifice breeding resentment toward others? Are you expecting others to give you the help and validation that only Christ can give? Are you busying yourself to the extent that you're forfeiting time with your Savior? Distance from Him clouds our eternal perspective. When we take our eyes off Him, we tend to put them on ourselves, and this self-absorption does not go well in any of our relationships.

It takes humility to repent of our demanding spirits and lay down what we feel like are our rights. Yes, parenting can drain us and leave us feeling like our resources are tapped out. But instead of demanding that others appreciate our level of sacrifice and in turn fill us back up, let's look to the Fountain of Living Water and gratefully trust in God's perfect provision.

> ## Father,
> Parenting is hard work! I knew this road wouldn't be easy, but I didn't expect the resentment I feel toward others because of my sacrifice. Forgive my self-absorption and pride, Father. Forgive my impure motives for serving, and forgive my demanding spirit. Help me to be humble and gracious. Let me be grateful for any help or friendship that is offered and not demand it in order to feel fulfilled. Thank You that You give me everything I need, in due time. Help me to choose the better thing—presence with You, a choice that results in a joyful servant's heart.

Day 27

CELEBRATE
THE SMALL THINGS

Give thanks in all circumstances.

—1 Thessalonians 5:18

The following scene plays out most days: My son stands in front of me, toe to toe, checking to see if today is the day. He stands on his tiptoes, and I tell him that's cheating. He puts on his shoes and tells me to take mine off; I tell him that is also cheating. Each time he checks I give the same answer: "Almost, but not yet." He groans. "One day you'll be taller than me," I say, "but today is not that day."

It's hard to tell you're growing when day-to-day progress is negligible. Miniscule growth is not the aim for my son where his height is concerned, or for any of us with regard to most goals. Yet by focusing only on whether or not we've met our larger objectives, we can neglect the smaller victories along the way.

We actually have a lot more reasons to celebrate than we think.

When we adopted Lucy at fifteen months old, she was the size and developmental age of a four-month-old. She'd never had anything to eat other than formula and rice cereal from a bottle, so she was terrified of a spoon, or anything else you tried to put in her mouth. There was so much ground to gain. The aim was to get her caught up in every way as soon as possible, but if we waited to celebrate until she met that goal, we would have missed out on lots of celebration-worthy steps along the way; moments such as . . .

The first time I wiped her mouth with a cloth and she didn't scream.

A full minute of tummy time without a tantrum.

Sitting up without falling to the side.

Holding a cracker in her hand.

Engaging with a toy.

We were ecstatic each time one of these itty-bitty milestones was reached, knowing they each pushed her one step closer toward the overarching goal of thriving health.

Our kids give us so many reasons to celebrate as they miraculously grow, trust, and eventually thrive. Miracles also occur within our own hearts as we learn to love well. I wonder: Do we slow down long enough to notice them? Do we celebrate our own growth and sanctification as we walk this parenting road?

Too often we miss our own progress because we're discouraged by our failures. But let me ask you: Did you patiently meet your child's need when you felt like you were all out of empathy? Victory. Did you repent after you responded to his need with frustration? Also a victory. Did you move toward your child with affection even though she stonewalled you? Victory. Did you beg the Lord to give you compassion when you felt cheated out of the love your child refused to give? Victory. Did you read one more story at bedtime even though your insides were screaming, "I just want to be done"? Victory. Were you convicted by your harshness at the end of the day, and did you go to your child and share how desperately you need Jesus too? Very much a victory.

You may not be the parent you want to be, but you're not the parent—or the person—you used to be, either. God is faithfully transforming you into His likeness because He promised to finish the work He started in you. Your growth may be miniscule; you may not have arrived at perfect patience or complete kindness, and you may not consistently respond with grace, but every day, there's progress. Each day, there's a little more Jesus and a little less you, whether you can see it for yourself or not. You can celebrate your sanctification in faith because God says maturity *is* happening. "For by one sacrifice he has made perfect forever those who are being made holy" (Hebrews 10:14). Positionally, before Him you are perfect because Christ's blood has made you clean. Relationally, He's changing your heart bit by bit, day by day, to be more like Him.

Isn't it wonderful that the same truth applies to our children? They are totally and completely ours from the minute we sign those papers—nothing can change their status in our family. And relationally, piece by piece, their hearts are being won over by love as they come to believe that they are cherished sons and daughters.

There is so much to celebrate.

You know, my Lucy is just as excited as her big brother about the prospect of growing, but she has a different perspective on the daily, albeit slow, progress. Each night she says, "If I go to sleep, my hair will grow, and I'll get big and strong!" Lucy closes her eyes in faith, and when she wakes in the morning, she cheers, "I got bigger! And my hair is longer!" She dances around the room, and we say, "Yay, Lucy! You're such a big girl!"

Instead of groaning over the progress she can't see, Lucy celebrates what she believes is happening—even though the change isn't obvious.

Perhaps we should follow her lead?

By faith, believe that you are being made new, whether you can see progress or not. Choose to believe that your child is growing and healing, even when major change is not obvious.

And throw a ridiculous party for all of the above because you have a Father who loves you enough not to leave you as you are.

Father,

You have given me so many reasons to celebrate. You came to earth as a man, lived the perfect life I could never live, and took the punishment I deserved. Not only have You given me the assurance of eternity with You, but You've also promised to change me to look more like You as I live my life here on earth. Just as I want to celebrate my children's baby steps toward health and wholeness, help me to remember to acknowledge and celebrate the work You're doing in my heart every day. I want to see less of me and more of You. Thank You for being committed to refine and sanctify me until I'm finally perfect in heaven with You.

Day 28

THOSE WHO ARE LEFT BEHIND

The LORD is close to the brokenhearted and saves those who are crushed in spirit.

—Psalm 34:18

*A*s I've mentioned before, my oldest daughter, Sarah Kate, loves stuffed animals. She can spot them a mile away, in all shapes and sizes, and wants them all to be her very own. It was no exception when she spied the cute little panda bears in traditional Chinese clothing at our hotel when we adopted Lucy. The hotel staff had given one to Lucy, and Sarah Kate begged us for one of her own. It was an easy yes.

Part of our breakfast routine each morning at the hotel became Sarah Kate checking the hotel gift shop to see how many pandas were left "waiting to be adopted," as she described it. She became super excited one day when there was only one left, but then was discouraged the next morning when there were three in the shop once again.

What Sarah Kate didn't realize was that the display window would never be empty because the hotel staff would simply replenish the stock each day. No matter how many families "adopted" the pandas, there would always be more to take their place. I didn't have the heart to tell her that there would always be pandas that needed homes, so I just let her rejoice when the count got low and ache when the display got full again.

My daughter was heartbroken over toys left in a gift shop. How much more devastating is the reality of the millions of children left in foster care, institutions, or simply on the streets? Once your heart has been turned inside out by the calling of adoption, you view the world through an entirely different lens. Your heart aches for the least of these like never before.

In his best-selling book *Radical*, David Platt says, "Orphans are easier to ignore before you know their names. They are easier to ignore before you see their faces. It is easier to pretend they're not real before you hold them in your arms. But once you do, everything changes."

Everything changes. Everything. When you've experienced the miracle of adoption, you can't simply scroll past the faces of waiting children on your newsfeed. When your heart has been split wide open with love you never knew was possible, you ache for those who have yet to know any form of love at all. When you've seen the transformation that a child undergoes when given a new name, family, and home, you weep for the little ones—and especially the big ones—who are shuffled from foster home to foster home, who wonder if anyone could ever want them.

We obviously can't bring all orphans home with us, as much as we wish we could, so what can we do? How can we best love those who have been left behind?

We give. We advocate. We educate those around us on the needs across the globe for families willing to open their hearts and their homes for one more. And we pray. We pray for a family coming soon for the ones who continue to wait, and we pray that in the meantime, they will physically feel the comforting arms of the only perfect Father.

The very best thing we can do is pray, so why don't we do that now?

Father,

My heart is breaking. While I rejoice at the opportunity to be family for even one of these treasures, I grieve for those who are left behind. I see them, God. I see their hungry faces and their empty eyes. I see their lifeless limbs, as they lie understimulated and underfed in stiff wooden cribs. I see their hearts grow another layer of cement as they're told they're moving to another foster home—again. I hear the newborn's cries for a mother that will not—cannot—come back. I want to be home for each of these children, but I know I physically can't.

God, will You be close to each of them tonight? As they toss fitfully into sleep without a goodnight kiss or a bedtime story, will You somehow whisper lullabies of love and presence?

God, will You speak words of worth and value to their hearts even now? When the enemy tries to tear them down with the emotional fallout of abandonment, when it seems that the world is against them, will You remind them that You are for them? Will You show them that they are perfectly and wonderfully made, and that Your dreams for them are so much greater than anything they could possibly conceive?

And Lord, please bring each of them a family. A home. Will You right now, at this very moment, stir the hearts of men and women around the globe to want to be mamas and daddies to these kids? If desires for security are stopping these kind people, then make them uncomfortable with comfort; let their appetites for ease somehow become distasteful. Break their hearts for the things that break Yours, God; we know that the plight of the fatherless is at the top of that list. Give these men and women courage to step out in faith and trust You for things they cannot see. For the money they can't imagine raising and the capacity they feel they do not have. As they learn of Your compassion, let their own compassion grow so that they will, by faith, step forward and say, "Yes." Show them that it's one of the best yeses they could possibly speak.

I trust You, Father, and I look forward to a day when there are orphans no more, and all are safely home.

Day 29

THE LUCKY ONES

*The LORD has done great things for us,
and we are filled with joy.*

—Psalm 126:3

I know they mean well. They always do. In fact, I should be grateful that their comments are encouraging, as opposed to being thoughtless or insensitive as others can be. Yet I cringe every time it happens because I just can't help it. I see the scenario coming a mile away: They glance at her and smile. They look up at me knowingly. *Here we go*, I think, as they open their mouths to speak those five well-intentioned words:

"What a lucky little girl."

I get what they're saying; I do. She now has a home, and a family who adores her. Her life trajectory is vastly different than what it would have been had she remained in the orphanage. She is blessed beyond measure because she has a mom and a dad and siblings who think she hung the moon. Yet I can't help but recoil inwardly because I know that the implications of that statement are all wrong.

First of all, we are not our children's saviors. We did not swoop down from our perfect lives and pluck them out of the pit. We don't demand that they be grateful. The truth is, for the millions of blessings that adoption brings, there is an undercurrent of loss. To go toward something, you must leave something behind, and even though life with us is immeasurably better than orphanages or foster care or no care at all, there was still a "life before"; there is a birth family. For internationally adopted kids, there was a native culture and language and foods. There may have been deep ties to foster parents.

Yes, our kids are blessed, but they have lost much as well. While we love them fiercely and would give our very lives for them, we are not rescuers; God is. We simply have the privilege of playing a small role in God's redemptive story.

The truth is, our children are not indebted to us in the least. If anything, we are indebted to them because we know who the lucky ones truly are: *us*.

It is an enormous privilege to be entrusted with such precious treasures. It is an incredible blessing to have a bird's-eye view of

God whittling away loss and exchanging ashes for beauty. We are honored that the Lord would love us enough to turn our worlds upside down and give us greater compassion and depths of love we did not know possible.

Every time that sweet hand reaches up to be held . . .

Each time she calls out, "Mama!" Every time he yells, "Daddy!" and runs into open arms . . .

With every milestone reached, every new nuance of trust and security, every smile offered that makes our hearts swell so big they just may leap out of our chests . . .

We know. We are the lucky ones.

The psalmist understands what an honor it is to not only be loved but also to be entrusted with caring for God's creation:

> *What is mankind that you are mindful of them,*
> *human beings that you care for them? You have made*
> *them a little lower than the angels and crowned them*
> *with glory and honor. You made them rulers over the*
> *works of your hands; You put everything under their*
> *feet: all flocks and herds, and the animals of the wild,*
> *the birds in the sky, and the fish in the sea, all that*
> *swim the paths of the seas. —Psalm 8:4–8*

The psalmist is overwhelmed by the blessings he's been given and he wonders, "Who am I?"

In our own context, we might say it something like this:

> *"God, who am I that You would entrust me with such a*
> *treasure, that You would call me, as imperfect and sinful as*
> *I am, to parent this one who is so dearly loved by You?"*

> *"God, who am I that You would love me enough*
> *to turn my world upside down? To strip me of deeply rooted*
> *idols of security and ease?"*

"God, who am I that You would seek to enlarge my view of the world, that You would gift me with compassion for the least of these?"

"God, who am I that You would allow me to identify with You through suffering?"

"God, who am I that You would give me a front-row seat to redemption?"

We can't even believe it. Our souls are filled to overflowing with gratefulness for His goodness to us in the form of little hands and feet, trust given and received, hearts softened by love.

What's my response when good, well-meaning people tell me how lucky my daughter is? Could I possibly explain the contradiction of loss and redemption, joy and pain? Dare I even try to scratch the surface of the unparalleled joy that being this little one's mother brings?

It isn't possible. I nod my thanks, I assume the best about their intentions, and often with misty eyes I say, "Oh no, I'm the lucky one," knowing that underneath my words are layers of meaning that I can't even begin to explain.

The Lord has done great things for us, and our hearts could not be filled with more delight.

Father,

I am incredibly blessed. Whatever amount of good that I have done for my child, it pales in comparison to the ways in which my child enriches my life. I am humbled that You would choose me to be this precious child's parent, that You would change me as You change my child. Thank You for the gifts of love and grace that You bestow on me through this priceless person every day. I know that my child is not lucky; instead, my child is chosen, redeemed, and dearly loved by You. And so am I. Thank You for entrusting me with this child's heart and life. I am forever grateful.

Day 30

HOME

*For [we are] looking forward to the city
with foundations, whose architect
and builder is God.*

—Hebrews 11:10

*H*ome. The very word triggers each of the senses: images of comfort and safety, smells of recipes tried and true, sounds of easy laughter and words of love, the feel of your comforter snuggled just right around your neck as you settle down for the night. Home is knowing and being known; it's belonging and security and rest.

In her essay, "In the Light of Home," Jennifer Trafton describes home as this:

....

Home is the place in the world that is both your soul's sanctuary and the anchor of your story, the place where the light slants on your life in such a way that all veils fall off, all shadows flee, and you can see your own face in the window merged with the world beyond.

....

Home is what we long to provide for our children as we endure the lengthy wait that separates us from them. It's something we will never again take for granted because we know it is not a guarantee for everyone. We have seen—we have lived—how the absence of home can drain the life out of a young soul. Home is what we dream of cultivating in hearts that have never known such a word. Sanctuary and story: we desire for both of these to come together under the roofs with which we shelter our young ones.

Sometimes they do. There are days and nights of laughter and belonging; there are seasons of affection and confident, quiet trust. We release a contented sigh, *Home. She knows that she's home; he is finally at ease in our care.*

As we create and enjoy home with our chosen ones, let's give thanks that the curtain has been pulled back and we have been given glimpses of the eternal home for which we were made. After all, those moments of rightness and belonging—they are but foreshadows of the home to come. God, in His goodness, allows us to breathe in the aroma of the hope of a forever home through every meal shared around the family table, every sleepy head nestled against Mom's shoulder, every giggle with Dad after lights out. "This is what we were made for," we whisper. *Home should always be this good.*

But sometimes the cracks in our earthly homes are exposed and the edges are rough. Sometimes days are long and tempers are short; grief cannot be consoled and pain is intense. Sometimes we reach the end of the day and the end of ourselves and we lament, "This is not the home I envisioned for my child. He deserves so much more than what I can give. *Home should not be this hard.*" And the enemy deceives. He discourages. He accuses with guilt and shame. He attempts to dissect the dream of home brick by brick.

Yet Paul assures us, "Where sin increased, grace increased all the more" (Romans 5:20).

When we are at the end of ourselves, He gives us more grace.

God reveals the cracks so we can more clearly see our need for Him. Instead of condemning us with shame, He uses the insufficiency of our imperfect homes to create in us a longing for the perfect home that is being prepared for us even now.

When tantrums fly and anger erupts, when we're too exhausted to engage meaningfully with our children, when home is more stressful than idyllic, it's a good thing that our souls cry, "*This is not how it should be.*" Because it isn't. God speaks through the chaos, "You are uncomfortable with the brokenness because you were made for another place."

And what a home that place will be! Can you even imagine it? Heaven will be the best parts of home multiplied to infinity— belonging and safety and perfect community, rest and relationship and peace. Home will then mean being fully known and fully loved with no reason to apologize or forgive, no baggage to carry. Home will be perfect communion with a perfect Father who is never annoyed or depleted and is always loving and good.

Are things going well in your home? Praise God that He is gifting You with a tiny taste of the home that is to come. Are the wheels falling off in the one place you want to feel whole? Does home feel less like a sanctuary and more like a battleground? Then praise God because when your soul is unsettled by the mess, you long all the more for your future perfect home. Let the cracks draw your family's eyes toward what is to come—"the city with foundations, whose architect and builder is God" (Hebrews 11:10).

On our very best days, let the magic of home whet our appetites for the home that will forever be satisfying and good. And on our very worst days, let our homes' inability to live up to our hearts' desires remind us that we're not actually home yet—but one day we will be, and we just can't wait to get there.

May gratitude and longing lead to worship.

Father,

You are home. The very best of home that I desire for my child pales in comparison with what You will one day provide. Help me to create the most nurturing home that I can for the time I have on earth—a home that will host love and instruction, affection and laughter. Security. Rest. When I experience those moments, let my very first thoughts be full of gratitude for the privilege of experiencing a taste of the home to come. And when my efforts fall short—and I know I constantly fall short—let the shortcomings of my home create in me a deep longing for my forever home with You.

Conclusion

To the weary adoptive parent, who thought everything was fine—until it wasn't.

Because of my friend Jill*, you, weary parent, have been on my mind. A lot. Jill attended a study of this very book, and if anyone was in need of hope, it was Jill. More than a decade ago, she and her husband flew across the globe to adopt their children as babies. They had the usual challenges that come with adoption, particularly international adoption, but in Jill's words, "Everything was great" . . . until the teen years. And now their lives have been turned upside down by identity issues and anger, resentment and confusion. The love their kids seemed to receive for years is now being rejected in ways Jill and her husband never anticipated. They never saw it coming, and now? They just don't know what to do.

It's been several years since I wrote the first edition of this book. My adopted daughter was a preschooler at the time. While my goal was to be honest and raw about my experience, specifically, and about the heartbreaking side of adoption in general, I've since heard Jill's story and so many others. While I know the truth in this book applies to the aching heart of every believing adoptive parent, I feel burdened to speak directly to you because I know the path you are walking is brutal.

I'm not where you are—not yet, at least—but I can imagine you feel alone. Blindsided. Maybe even betrayed. The one for whom you have laid down your life, who you love with your whole being and who once loved you back, is now not so sure. Maybe they're making decisions that are harmful, and you have no idea how to pull them back from what feels like disaster.

I can only imagine the weight of such unbearable grief.

Oh, friend. I wish I could speak to you face-to-face. I wish you could see the tears in my eyes. Since you can't, please hear me speak to you—just to you. You are seen. You are not alone. You are held. You are not forgotten—and neither is your child. Not now, not ever.

In a particularly low moment in my own life, a friend sent me some much-needed encouragement. Maybe you need to hear it today:

"The Lord is with you, and He is working for His name's sake, strengthening your weak arms and feeble knees by confessing your disappointment, weakness, anger, anguish, and doubt. Cry out to the One who has saved us from the consequences of our sin and will bring us into a home filled with many rooms, a feast and a throne. There are clouds of witnesses above and around you urging you on. They too have suffered and overcome and are now reaping their rewards. Consider them, consider Christ who had just 'one more mile to go' when beaten and bloodied, then had to drag His Cross uphill and be nailed to it before it was finished. For the joy set before Him, He endured the Cross, scorning its shame. Keep going."

Keep going. Please keep going. Keep putting one foot in front of the other, as you love, obey, and hope—not in changed circumstances but in the One who never changes. Fight to keep your own heart soft when all it wants to do is shut down and self-protect. I know it's tempting to numb the pain, but if you shut down your heart, you'll miss out on the good stuff too. Believe it or not, there is joy to be found, even in this dark place. God says so:

I will give you hidden treasures, riches stored in secret
places, so that you may know that I am the LORD,
the God of Israel, who summons you by name.
—Isaiah 45:3

Do you hear Him gently calling you by name? He wants you to know that He is faithful. Your labor has not been in vain, no matter what the fruit of your labor looks like today, tomorrow, or ten years from now. For the joy set before you, for the sake of the kingdom, for the treasures God has for you and your child in this life and the next, keep going. *It's still worth it.*

Much love,
Jennifer

*not her real name

If you enjoyed this book, will you consider sharing the message with others?

Let us know your thoughts at info@newhopepublishers.com. You can also let the author know by visiting or sharing a photo of the cover on our social media pages or leaving a review at a retailer's site. All of it helps us get the message out!

Twitter.com/NewHopeBooks

Facebook.com/NewHopePublishers

Instagram.com/NewHopePublishers

————————

New Hope® Publishers, Ascender Books, Iron Stream Books, and New Hope Kidz are imprints of Iron Stream Media, which derives its name from Proverbs 27:17, "As iron sharpens iron, so one person sharpens another."

This sharpening describes the process of discipleship, one to another. With this in mind, Iron Stream Media provides a variety of solutions for churches, ministry leaders, and nonprofits ranging from in-depth Bible study curriculum and Christian book publishing to custom publishing and consultative services. Through the popular Life Bible Study and Student Life Bible Study brands, ISM provides web-based full-year and short-term Bible study teaching plans as well as printed devotionals, Bibles, and discipleship curriculum.

For more information on ISM and New Hope Publishers, please visit

IronStreamMedia.com

NewHopePublishers.com